To
Val
x

BOB MADDOCKS

It's Unbelievable Really

Bob

JELLY BEAN BOOKS · CARDIFF
2025

Bob Maddocks: It's Unbelievable Really 2025

Jelly Bean Books
Mackintosh House
136 Newport Road
Cardiff Road
CF24 1DJ

www.candyjarbooks.co.uk

Printed and bound by
4edge, 22 Eldon Way, Hockley, Essex, SS5 4AD

ISBN: 978-1-917022-64-4

Introduction

Bob Maddocks is an ordinary man, yet an extraordinary man.

He has lived through the second half of the twentieth century and the first quarter of the twenty-first. Times that have seen remarkable changes in the fabric of British society and in the attitudes and expectations that have accompanied those changes.

Throughout his life, however, Bob's focus has been consistent: get on with what needs to be done, make the most of any situation and give your best to help and support others, especially those closest to you. In those respects, Bob represents both the greatest attributes of the society he grew up in and the finest qualities of the society of today.

In the autobiography that follows [with the exception of his earliest years as a child during World War II], there are no earth-shatteringly famous events of national or global significance to recount and, although so much has changed during Bob's eighty-four years on the planet, like the vast majority of people everywhere, Bob's life story is much more about the everyday challenges that truly dominate our lives.

That is what makes this book such a fascinating insight into history. It is essentially a series of vignettes, all recounting Bob's ability to cope with whatever comes his way. At times his coping mechanism is to move on to pastures new, but this is motivated less by a desire to escape the status quo and more from an insatiable wanderlust and a willingness to try again and experience new things.

There are struggles, mistakes, hardships and losses, but equally there is immense humour, fortitude and courage on display, making Bob's life-time of stories a rollercoaster ride through the chaos of real life that is sure to delight and entertain the reader.

Ultimately, the overriding message is one of self-reliance and adaptability, in a story that offers both a nostalgic trip down memory lane for readers of Bob's generation, but also a timely lesson for today's society that honesty, self-respect and a willingness to embrace the demands of an ever changing world, can help us all to live an interesting, meaningful and rewarding life.

Prologue

I'm sitting this evening in Cowbridge in The Duke of Wellington, and I'm going to explain my whole life.

I'm eighty-four and my memory is not all it once was, so I want to get all this history down now, while I still can. I've made a list of all the places I've lived in my life, and there have been quite a few… which provides useful points of reference and, I believe, is reasonably accurate.

Some of my account may be lacking in specifics and, because I'm recording these memoirs, while having a conversation in the pub, I might sometimes repeat things, or go off on a tangent, or just ramble on now and then. But that's how we all talk when chatting in the pub and I hope that by retaining that sense of having a conversation with me, as you read what follows, you'll hear my voice in the words on the page.

I've done this chiefly because I think I've had a reasonably interesting life and I'd like my family and future generations to have a written account of it. Like all autobiographical accounts, it may be a tad self-indulgent here and there, but I've sought to be factual and I've tried hard to get the names of people and places right.

Descriptions of events are unembellished. You might

not always find that entirely credible, but my life has often been chaotic – perhaps it all has; hence the title of this book. But trust me: it's all true!

Chapter One
Boy to Man

1940 – 1958
"I shan't be back tomorrow"

I was born in Penarth, Glamorgan on 9th March, 1940 at number 30 Plassey St, which was a small place.

I reckon I was only a few months old when I moved to a place called Maughan Terrace, which is about half a mile away. I remember most of my upbringing from there and lived in the same house until I was eleven years old.

I don't have many memories of my earliest years, even though the war was on. The Germans were bombing Cardiff Docks, and I think St Augustine's Church, which was near to us, served as a kind of landmark for them to drop their bombs. I only remember a lot of noise: banging and flashing and the air raid warnings. There was a lot of fog in those days, or smog, because of all the coal fires. I do remember once seeing an effigy of Mussolini hanging upside down on a lamppost. We were kids of course, so I didn't know what it was about. I had no idea who Mussolini was. To me, it just looked like a Guy Fawkes.

We lived near the docks and I remember seeing a lot of American troops on the streets. What was it people used to say about them? "Over-sexed, overpaid and over here." I do remember that they were often black and, most probably, from poor backgrounds. They looked rich to us though in their Army and Navy uniforms. After the war, some brides did go to the US and were horrified to discover where their husbands lived. A lot of them came back.

There was a lot of friction with the Americans in the pubs. I was, of course, too young to go in the pubs, but people were talking about it all the time.

I never went into an air raid shelter. We were told to get under the table, and that's what we did. We used to make dens under there. It was laughable really because Maughan Terrace was falling down anyway. The joke used to be: if the bombers flew over our house and looked down they'd think they'd bombed there already. They were horrible terraced houses, divided into flats, on the hill. The roof was actually hanging off ours, but we stayed there for a decade.

We rented it. The landlord was a Mr Bryant. He used to come round every week with his bag. I remember all that. We lived in the top flat. The people downstairs had a garden. My father was a keen gardener and he wanted the downstairs, so he could do the garden. Eventually we did swap with the Forsyths, downstairs. They emigrated to Australia in 1950 something. Their son Alan and I went to cubs and scouts together in little hats and uniforms. He was two years older than me.

"Be Prepared," they used to say. But I've not been prepared all my life.

When you start out, other people's lives seem better than what you have. Their houses, for instance, seem cleaner or bigger, but this is often not true. All you need to do is look below the surface. I was lucky to have a very good mother. My earliest memory was when I was five or six; nothing before, the years before that are blanked out. My wife Ruth has memories of when she was three and four, but I haven't. Ruth lived in Paget Place, right next to the docks and she said the tanks used to go past her house. I was in the next street up, so I didn't see any of that.

My earliest clear memory is coming down the hill from

school. It was 1946, and I saw a pram outside our house. My sister had been born and that was the first time I'd ever seen a baby. My mother was quite blunt about it.

'Robert, that's your new sister,' she said.

But I don't have an old one, I remember thinking.

My sister and I were both very shy and quiet. I think we were both subdued by something heavy hanging over us

Despite this, we were quite happy there. I particularly remember the winter of 1947 when we had heavy snow. The kids got their toboggans out and we used to have great fun there, causing mayhem for the poor old bus drivers. We'd come down the hill from St Augustine's (which was the highest part) on these bloody stupid toboggans. We'd then go down Maughan Terrace, turn left, down the dock road, right down to the beach, flying across the road in front of the bus – all the way down, but we didn't care. We crossed two junctions where the poor buses were coming along. If it wasn't for the sea, we would have kept going. Mind you, it was a long way back up then. The council would put grit down of course, but we were quite happy to scoop it back up. Our games were more important.

My earliest memory of my infant school in Albert Road was going up the road and meeting other young people like myself. I was very self-conscious and perhaps a bit shy. The first teacher I remember was a Miss Warne, a very Victorian lady; a fifty-ish-year-old spinster, I think. I was terrified when I first saw her, but soon warmed to her. She was a good teacher and I spent most of my primary school years with her as my form teacher. She was definitely instrumental in my success later, particularly my getting into grammar school.

There were a couple of boys in our class from the Gibbs Home. They weren't rough exactly, but they had no interest at all in studying. I sat with them and we had one book between the three of us sometimes. Sometimes they would smell and I would move away from them if the pong got too pungent.

When we read, Ms Warne would stand behind your

shoulder. At my turn, I would try and get my line out quickly before she asked me for it. I was too fast really. I remember her asking me about a granary, near the harbour. She asked what a granary was, but almost before she'd got the question out, I fired off the answer, 'astorehouseforgrain,' almost just like that. Fast. She used to tell us stories and they all became fixed in my head, because I loved that.

One year she introduced a crafting project: we had to make something. I didn't know what to do, but, of course, everyone had ration books then and she suggested I make a ration book holder. I asked her what I could make that out of, but she said: anything. Well, it's not very exciting, is it? I said that to her too, but she said I should just do it. We tried to sell the items we'd made. Well, as you can imagine, nobody bought it. It went in the dump. It reminds me of someone I knew later in life: an artist who used to bring her stuff into the pub to sell… and nobody ever bought any of that; it was awful.

During morning assembly, we used to sing all the usual songs, and she'd be looking around the class; there were thirty of us. She'd glare at me and call me by my surname; she'd call me "Maddocks" and she focused on me for some reason, while I was singing, which I hated.

'Maddocks, don't sing, don't sing,' she would say.

Well, that cuts you down a bit. I was looking around and they were all looking at me. Then she said, 'You can sing, but don't sing. Pretend to be singing… just mime the words.'

Okay, I'll mime the words, I thought, trying to look serious. The problem was, the first time I mimed the words, the whole bloody class collapsed. The first one who laughed nearly fell of his chair. Of course, I didn't mean it to be funny, but she'd made it happen, so they all cracked up. They stopped singing.

'You can start singing again, as this is causing chaos, but don't sing loud,' she said crossly.

It wasn't my fault, but I thought, *Okay, sure.*

I told her later, 'Shirley Bassey was told the same thing in Splott, in Cardiff, when she was ten.' Isn't it amazing how you can be put down, early on in life?

Anyway, I was looking around the class at the other kids, and they all seemed brighter than me. There were some idiots: there were two brothers called Donald and David Hoare – they were thick as two short planks. But I got to a point where I was very good at English. My maths was appalling, but somehow I came top once. Because of this I was told to go up and do it on the board. Well, it was all Greek to me. I struggled to get through it and was all embarrassed.

I was very young and silly. We did this thing one day. I was maybe nine or ten. They'd make you get up on a stage, on a platform and say, 'Imagine you're on a fishing boat and you're fishing.'

There's nothing in front of you. You've got nothing except your imagination. I had a riot with that. I got up on the stage, with everyone waiting, and all the class staring at me. I felt nervous and I blushed. I was shy and this was quite a physical thing. But once I got on up there something happened – a tingling sensation and I calmed down. I looked at all the people and realised they were there to be entertained. Suddenly I realised I was in charge. It's hard to explain.

For a second I went into a world of my own and they said, 'Get on with it. Pretend you're on a rock.'

So I sat down, imagining a seat. I remember it vividly. In my mind I created an imaginary stool. I remember all my class looking at me, all sat there. I produced an imaginary rod and cast it out into an imaginary ocean. I was very self-conscious for the first few seconds, but then I got into it. I started to bring the fish in, taking each one off the hook. My class were all mesmerised. I was into it and they wanted me to do more.

The teacher then said, 'That's enough, that's enough."

And she pulls me off the stage. But this makes you popular, and when you're popular (and cause laughter) you get away with things.

I remember visiting the local docks. It was a bit run-down, with two old steel-hulled ships in the harbour called Palmire and Passat. These were old, ocean-going sailing ships that were now moored up there. They'd come to the end of their life, because steam had taken over. I was quite interested in ships and, after the war, lots of other ships had been mothballed in Penarth Docks.

There were dozens of them, all these grey ships lined up. We used to play on them. They made a great playground. I remember the local docks' policeman. He was retired from the army and was known as Lockjaw. He'd been in the war, poor man. He used to chase us off, but we just kept going back on other boats. To me, well I was so young, it was just a playground for us.

Everyone was going down there, swimming in the docks. Of course, in those days, the sea used to come right in. They've built the barrage since then, but the tide used to come in and go out twice a day. We used to jump off the piers and swim out in the docks. The docks weren't so busy. It was all closing down and quite quiet in my time. Cardiff Docks were still busy, but Penarth Docks had become more of a mooring place.

There were also lots of abandoned buildings, so the docks were really just a playground. The trams and trains had gone. I've got a picture somewhere and there's just nothing there – desolate, overgrown with brambles, but it was a playground for kids that was amazing. We shot catapults there at God-knows-what. It's played a most important part in my life: being near the sea all the time.

I had a small rowing boat, which was given to me to play with, not at sea, but on the river Ely, on the channel where the tide came in and went out. We all went fishing and were always running about, keeping ourselves busy.

There was a chap called Michael Downs, who later went into the Royal Navy. He was my age. He was called Dripper Downs, and he answered to the name Dripper. We used to play hide-and-seek and he used to go and hide behind the lamppost. It's just little things that kids say. His father, Mr Downs, used to play football in the street with us too and come down and talk to me. My father didn't play football in the street. He just had me running errands, running about like a bloody idiot.

I'll tell you a story about a girlfriend I had later on. She used to come home from her school in Penarth, the Catholic one. Michael Downs was at the same school. She'd been about ten or eleven then, I think. Apparently, he'd annoyed her so much, by pulling her pigtails more than once, that she whipped him with her skipping rope. He told me this… and that was my future wife! She'd whacked him and he'd run off. Then some woman had told her off for hitting this boy, saying that it wasn't the first time she'd seen others hitting Michael. She wondered what we had against him. But, it was just life, going on. You can be bullied all your life, can't you? Girls are often worse, but if you hit out, you get the stick in school.

My father was a horrible man. I'll say that now. He was a man who did not like me, who wasn't interested in me. I seemed to be not what he wanted. I don't know what was wrong with him. Of course, when you're young, there are a lot of people around, all talking to you. Growing up in the war years, everyone was very busy. I used to visit my grandparents quite a lot, but there's a big gap in my history from ages one 'til four. I think I know why. Although I don't remember it, my sister told me later that when I was very young, my father used to beat me and kick me.

I can't really explain why my father was like this. I just realised that something was not quite right. And my mother would call him "Father", which was strange. When he would come up the road, on his way home from work, the whole atmosphere of the house changed and she would go into a panic mode.

He worked in Cardiff Docks. A blacksmith's striker, he was, and very good at that. He was also good at fishing and gardening and had allotments. I was no good at that and I was a great disappointment to him.

He even had a fishing boat called Girl Pat. I say a "fishing" boat – it was a boat, moored on the river Ely. He used to go fishing every other day, whenever the tide came in. It could be half past three in the morning, but he'd get out of bed and go fishing. I wasn't interested in fishing at half past three in the morning. I was bloody cold and I had school to go to in the morning, didn't I? But I had to go along with it, I wasn't given a choice. There was no argument about it, but I didn't like it. I did it throughout my childhood, even though I couldn't even take a fish off a hook. I was too squeamish.

But my grandfather, whose name was Bill, looked out for me. One day, getting on the boat, I was carrying the tea in a thermos and I dropped it and the tea spilled everywhere. My grandfather took it from me and refilled it with hot water and tea before my dad got on the boat. He came on and said he'd have a cup of tea and grabbed the flask. 'Christ, that's hot,' he said, and my grandfather replied that maybe we needed a new flask. He was protecting me from my dad. They hated each other. I could see the hostility, even though I was only young, and of course it all got absorbed into my brain, but when you're young, you don't ask too many questions.

My grandfather is long gone now, but he used to always come out on the boat with us. One day we were out at Flat or Steep Holm. My dad and my grandad were arguing about something; Well, they were always arguing.

'We'll go back now,' my grandad said.

The tide was turning. When it turns it goes out rapidly and the Cardiff entrance becomes just mud. It's amazing.

Just sheer mud! So, we were coming back and we could see the docks, cos they were open then. They're not anymore. Well, we were going to go up the River Ely, but we didn't get there. The boat started slowing down and we were hitting the mud. And we stopped. This was half past evening time… whatever time it was, but late!

'My god!' my grandfather was shouting. 'We are stuck now and the tide is still going out.' As it goes out, it's like you're on a cliff. I mean, we could have gone sliding around forever. I was just a kid, so blameless. Anyway, we had to stay there until the tide turned again and that took a long time. It must have been at the weekend because I didn't get to school on Monday.

You can imagine it, can't you? 'Sorry, teacher, we were stuck on the mud.'

When the tide came in, I remember it vividly. They were rocking the boat and the suction from the mud was so considerable that the boat didn't move for a few minutes. Then I saw the water coming up the side. So, as the water came up, they started rocking the boat to release it. Then, the bloody engine wouldn't start.

They got it going eventually and we got back in. Can you imagine? I was blue. When I eventually got back into school, they asked me what I'd done on the weekend and I had to write an essay all about it. Unbelievable!

The eleven-plus came up and I passed. I didn't pass in Maths though. I failed that every time, but I must have passed in general English, and I got to Grammar School. This was surprising because we didn't really have any books in our house. We had some on flowers and plants because my father was interested in all that, but there was nothing for me to read. It's funny though. I remember a few things that stick in my head like the book, *For Whom the Bell Tolls*. I think Hemmingway wrote it and it might have been about the Spanish Civil War. But chiefly I remember the lines: "Ask not for whom the bell tolls, it tolls for thee." It's funny what sticks in your head.

The eleven-plus test was all on one paper. It was a series of questions including English, Maths and general knowledge. It was a big day, that was. They lined us up in the yard in the morning and told us who was going to Grammar school and who was not. The alternative, the abyss that it was, was called Cogan, down the road you see, and I thought, *I don't want to go there.* But I passed and then, went home, told my mother. Father wasn't interested, but mother was over the moon.

Chapter Two
Grammar School Years

My mother had to find the money to pay for my uniform. We were poor you see. We'd moved to a house in St Augustine's Road, but still rented. My father was working on the docks. Anyway, we went into town and my mother had a provincial cheque – a loan provided by an insurance company for ten or twelve pounds. You received the money and paid it back over ten weeks. I'm sure that this was a tremendous burden for my mother. Despite this, we went into the shop in Windsor Road in Penarth, and I went to grammar school in a brand new uniform, cap and suit.

I thought, *Here we go again.* I was going to a new school and, to be honest, I was terrified. I didn't know what to do. I felt that I should have gone to the other school.

I also had a plastic satchel, which fell apart. The others all seemed to have leather, so I felt slightly inferior. I wasn't, but that's how I felt.

Anyway, I was very good at sports including rugby, swimming, running and javelin throwing. It was sport that got me through it really. I was useless at maths, but good at English and French. I could understand it and this brought me out of my shell a bit. I don't know what it was, but I had something they didn't have and I became very popular. I didn't intend this, of course. I wanted to keep out of the way, but these things happen.

Nevertheless, I wasn't very happy at school and I kept looking out the window. I was forever getting caught out. I remember thinking, *I don't like this*. But my mother was so proud of me. 'Robert has gone to grammar school,' she kept saying.

I went back to the house one night and there were about ten women in the front room.

Mum said, 'Oh, do you know Robert's gone to Grammar School?'

They replied, 'Yes, May, you've told everyone in the entire village.'

My mother had been abandoned as a child. Her own mother left her at a home in Aberdare. She knew people there called Jack and Muriel. Muriel had been her friend at the home and Jack was Muriel's husband. I remember going there on holiday. It was 8 Miners Road if my memory serves me correct. It's strange how things go around in life. To think that my granddaughter would later be abandoned. It's strange how life does this. Thinking back, other parents used to say that I had more sense than their sons. I don't know if that's true. I guess I was old before my time.

The one thing I remember, though, is that my mother was proud of me. Most of the kids in my area didn't go to grammar school. They went to Cogan, the place where I should have gone. Sadly my grammar school didn't really prepare me for the future.

I liked carpentry and the teacher was called 'Big Bill'. In his class he'd line us up, with all the tools set out on this beautiful bench. It was polished mahogany, but he wouldn't let us touch it. As you can imagine, I didn't learn a lot about carpentry. This strange because in later life I became an antique restorer, working with wood. Sometimes you just feel short-changed by education.

I remember getting the cane in school. I could be naughty, but most of the time I was quite a soft, easy-going guy. Saying that, if someone hit and kicked me, I hit back. I once had six of the best for hitting a boy, who had hit me first. We used to get whacked on the hand and this really hurt. People today don't realise. Back in those days, it was acceptable to use the cane or stick. I didn't agree with this though. The unfairness of it used to make me angry. It could break your fingers, but they didn't care. The teachers couldn't care less and neither did the headmaster. I guess that's life.

Penarth County Grammar School did not bring out the best in people. It was too academic. I didn't actually like the school, but I got on with one or two of the teachers, like Mr Ellis in French and Geography. I hated Maths and music. I'm sure the music teacher must have despaired of me. I thought I was the odd person out, although people did keep coming to me for things.

We went on school trips. We used to go to Chepstow quite a bit. We'd go on the bus and then walk around Tintern Abbey and go home. It was boring as hell. The teaching methods in grammar school were not the best. Like I said, I would stare out of the classroom window sometimes. I remember one day, hearing my name called. 'Maddocks, wake up!'

I turned around and, in the way that only teachers speak, I was asked to explain something: 'Maddocks, could you just elucidate on the so and so of the so and so…'

I thought, *Jesus Christ, I don't know what he's talking about.*

So I used to make it up, didn't I? By making it up, it brought humour into the situation. I didn't really understand this then, but as I went through life, I realised that humour can take you away from a problem. When you get people laughing, they lose their control over you.

After school, I had a paper round. It started at half past four, followed by errands for my father. I'd saved up £1 a week for a bike. I bought it from Greys in Grove Terrace. I used to deliver the *South Wales Echo*. I used to pick up sixty-seven papers to deliver from Glebe Street in Penarth. Off I'd go, rain or shine. On a Friday evening, they would pay us, maybe tuppence a week. Some people used to take advantage and say, 'Oh, Robert, while you're here, could you nip down and get me some bread or cheese from the shops?'

I would think, *I'm on a paper round here. I can't be diving off. I'll never get finished.* But it happened and I just used to say, 'Oh… yes, yes, yes.'

I'd normally get home at half past six, half past seven sometimes. After my homework, my day was gone. But I didn't mind, I met some interesting people. My mate Bobby Curren, who lived in the house next door, had the round before me. He said to be careful of two women at the bottom of the road, whose husbands were airline pilots. He warned me that they were a bit 'too sexy'! There was lots of innuendo flying around and, I must admit, I didn't quite realise this at twelve, thirteen and fourteen.

Regularly I would visit one particular address: 9 Paget Terrace in Penarth. This lady paid me one and threepence when I was twelve. I thought she was a lovely lady. She was a stern Victorian lady, and I was quite frightened of her. I did, however, like the one and threepence she used to give me every Friday. That was a tuppence tip! I wonder if she ever thought that one day I'd be calling on her to marry her daughter!

In those days, the houses had long corridors, and when I looked behind her, I saw this girl in the background. It wasn't Ruth. It was another girl – her sister. When I was at that door, she used to scuttle up the stairs. I remember that.

I used to call on my grandparents after my paper round almost every day. They were very close to me. Gran and Gramps, I called them. They lived on the ground floor of a house at 47 Maughan Street. My grandfather used to be on the Windjammers, the sailing ships. The Clippers on the Australian run. Those ships relied on the wind, transporting goods from England to Australia. They were known as Windjammers because that's how they got to where they were going. It would take roughly three months to get to Australia from Britain. The runs were very fast, but on every trip, they'd lose one of the crew. Gramps used to tell me about that. They'd fall off the rigging, when the ship was turning to port or starboard, and end up in the sea. They'd be gone then, but sometimes they also hit the deck. It was a hard life, managing heavy, salt-laden sails. So hard! They had to be fit and healthy, and they were quite cheerful people, singing sea shanties and stuff.

Gramps was, what you'd call an old sea dog, and his stories used to get into my head. He told me that on a ship you had to look after yourself and be responsible. He inspired me a lot and I used to listen carefully to him. I remember watching him very carefully in the kitchen. He had fingers missing and no fingernails left because of the canvas. He looked a hundred and four, but he was only about sixty. He was a hard man.

My grandmother used to make tea for me. She was a very hard-working lady – a washerwoman. But there was no love lost between my grandparents and my father. This was quite obvious. Once I went on an errand for my father, who'd given me ten shillings to get him some Woodbines. I was very young, maybe ten or eleven. I came out of the shop and I didn't know where the change had gone. I went to Gramps and I was crying. He asked me what the matter was and I explained I hadn't got the change. I said I didn't know how it had happened. It was just one of those things. He just gave me the money; to make it right, and he didn't tell my father. He was very protective, he was. He told my future girlfriend, 'Whatever Robert does is all right by us.' But I'm jumping ahead now.

Looking back now I realise, I liked them and they liked me.

Now, my grandad was in 'Dad's Army', as they called it: The Home Guard. He had a Home Guard jacket, which he cut down and gave me later for working in the cold mornings. So I'd walk down the road with a Home Guard top on. He was a great, great man, but my father didn't like him. He hated him. My dad used to say, 'Before we go fishing tomorrow, we won't call Grandad.' This was his *own* dad.

But Gramps would be down on his boat at 2am, with the kettle going. This would be long before my dad had even got out of bed. Basically, when the tide turned, he was there. We'd get there and my dad would just say, 'Oh, you're here.'

My grandparents had two sons, Vivian Harry Maddocks, and my father, William John Edward Maddocks. I remember a conversation about my uncle who had died in the war. Gran was in the kitchen in Maughan Street and I remember her saying to Ruth, 'The wrong one died in the war.'

It was obvious something was going on, but I didn't ask what she meant.

Ruth later asked, 'What did she say?'

I thought perhaps I'd misheard it, but Ruth repeated it. She was horrified. I couldn't believe Gran had said it, but she did. It was obvious that she didn't like my father and he didn't like me or my mother. I won't go into that any further.

My uncle died on HMS Glorious, when it was sunk during the war, off Norway.

He was twenty-one. I've got photos of him. There was definitely something going on there, but I didn't understand. Skeletons in the cupboard.

My sister used to say, 'Why is that picture in our front room of our mother and Uncle Harry?'

It was on the mantelpiece over the fireplace. My uncle was in full uniform and his was standing with my mother. Oddly my father was not there. There have been a lot of remarks about it over the years. I can't know for certain what happened, but during the war years a baby was born. That was me. Harry went off to sea and got killed and so, I suppose, the other brother married my mum. I think that's why he had something over her. She was in fear of him. When she was young, she used to go out and play the piano and enjoy herself and Harry did too. But my father just didn't go out. He was a miserable bugger and horrible with it.

My sister now owns that picture. Uncle Harry is in his HMS Glorious uniform, although the 'Glorious' has been cut off his shirt. During the war, you would never take a photo that revealed the ship you were on. It just says HMS. He left me one of his HMS Glorious caps, or it was left to me by somebody. But, at a street party in 1947, some woman stole it. It wasn't worth anything.

My mother used to look after the house. She was a good parent. She used to bring people around just before 3pm at Maughan Terrace. And when I arrived home from school, there'd be a party in the front room and Mother would be reading the tea leaves. You know, taking the tea cups and up-ending them. I used to watch my mother do it, and she had those people believing her, and more often than not, she was right!

Mother tried to palm me off once with this poor girl called Jean Wallace. Poor bugger. They were all in it together. These women kept telling her, 'Oh, he'll do for you.'

We were sat in the kitchen and Jean was prepared to talk, but I was so embarrassed I couldn't even speak, and I had to escape. I didn't know what to do. I left the room, and I didn't go back. What must she have thought of me?

But at 4.45pm… panic! My sister used to tell me tales about it later. She said that my father used to kick me, which I didn't believe. Why would he kick me? Didn't he like me?

And my sister also said that one time my mother decided to leave home. She walked off up the road with my sister. Well, my father followed her and called her back.

Then there was a Mr Drew, an insurance man. He was very dapper, but had lost his wife. He used to call round every Friday for the insurance policies. They were called penny policies in those times. My mother had so many, which is why she had to see him. He was very polite. He used to doff his hat when he came in. He wanted someone to look after him and his children. He asked my mother to run away with him.

My father was a hard-working man. He worked on the docks in Mount Stuart Docks, Cardiff. I've got pictures of him. It was heavy, heavy work. He used to cycle there and cycle home. It was rough and he was a hard man. He made everything in iron and steel like anchor chains and heavy machinery. It was a big, heavy job. The ships were always going in for repairs though. His wage was £7 a week. At the time, we didn't really know what he was on, because he would tear the packet open before he got home. He'd take out money for himself, for cigarettes and beer and give my mother the balance, so we never knew what he earned, but it was roughly £7 a week. He might have been on £9, but there it is.

During the war, he worked as a fireman. He didn't go into action because being a fireman was protected work. He'd also worked in a fish place in Penarth. I believe there was a problem with someone there, or something went wrong there. Apparently, it ended up with a knife being drawn. It's little things, but it ended up with him moving on. He wasn't very popular, my father. Unless he was in the pub and was very popular then!

Back then, in Penarth, he visited The Clive Arms, the only pub not on a corner in Johns Street, as well as The Pilot Hotel, where I later worked for a year (another story), The Red Lion, The Albion, The Labour Club and The Social Club at St Fagan's.

When I got older, and I went out on a Saturday night, I'd start off in the pubs, drinking a half of this and a half of that, and by the time I got to the dancehall, I was beyond recognition – pissed is the word. I was just trying to get up some Dutch courage to dance with people. I didn't know what to do with a girl when I was young!

As a teenager, in the '50s, I was a very good swimmer, very athletic. I could run and run and not get out of breath – something to do with a low blood count or low blood pressure. Sebastian Coe has the same, I'm told. Your pulse rate is very slow and it goes down. It's a problem now, if it gets too low, I'm knackered. But I could run, and I used to think it was almost insulting as I ran on, to be passing someone gasping for breath. I had some ability, but I never did anything with it.

I used to run errands for people. I'd often bring scrap home from the docks for my father.

Everybody went swimming, twice a day. It was just keeping fit, and it was cheap as well. We called the place The Baths. It was nothing exciting, just a council-maintained place. It was on the Esplanade in Penarth and was pretty horrible. A council worker used to be there in boots and dungarees with a net, sweeping up all the rubbish off the water's surface. There was loads of chlorine in the water, horrible stuff. You used to rinse it out when you got out. But these were happy days, with everybody doing the same thing. Real life – everyday life was the biggest influence on our lives – not celebrities, or anything like that.

Later, I would spend my time on my motorbike, going as far as my petrol would take me. I got my first bike in '57, when I was seventeen. It was a Triumph Tiger Cub, a 199C. It arrived at Penarth Railway Station in a package and wasn't driveable. I'd saved up for that and paid cash. It came, I remember, from a company called Kings in Oxford. The company's probably still there. I used to wait for the bike every day at the railway station. The guard got to know me and on the day it arrived he gave me this wrapped-up package and I asked, 'What am I going to do with that?'

'It's up to you,' he replied. I removed all the wrapping and left all that on the station. He didn't like that, but he was all right. I managed to free the handlebars and straighten them out and I pushed that bike from the station all the way up St Augustine's Hill. It was exhausting. Soon I got it going and off I went, nearly killing myself. But thankfully I survived.

It lasted me less than six or seven months. I was working as a fitter or a mechanic's helper at a place called Ross Garages on Penarth Road. Ross Garages was a big name. They were run by a Jewish family. I had three or four jobs in the space of a year. I remember working there as a helper or fitter, but I didn't really have any idea what I was doing. I had no idea about spanners and numbers. I do remember I parked my Tiger Cub outside there one morning and a bloke came along with a Triumph Tiger 110. Bloody hell! He parked alongside mine and mine looked small. I thought sod that, went straight into town and got myself a Tiger 110.

I think I had the bikes at the same time as I was working at sea and used them in between voyages. I remember when I was away one time, the payments on the bike stopped and they came and took it away. We were still living in St Augustine's Road then. I was so busy and doing so many things, I wasn't focused on any one thing and my life was going in all ways. When you're young you can drop one job and go and start another the next day. Other people leave school, go to university then have one job all their lives. There's nothing wrong with that, but I wouldn't have much to talk about if I'd done that.

Chapter Three
Girlfriends and Neighbours

Around the same time, I started dating Ruth. She was the first girl I brought back to the house. I was embarrassed to bring her home because of my father. My mother was on edge. He was so rude. This was at St. Augustine's Road, number 15. We lived downstairs mostly in the basement where the kitchen was, because the rest of the house was so cold. We all stayed in the kitchen. That's where the fire was.

As soon my father arrived, the temperature went right down. He'd come in the house and I'd be thinking, *Oh my God! I want to impress my girlfriend.* But he'd come down the stairs and… grunt! I was paranoid with fear. We never got through the tea, as he would look to the side and grunt again. Or, maybe he'd make a remark to my mother.

He came back from Cardiff once on the same bus as Ruth. There were only the two of them on the bus, but he ignored her. Then he walked from the bus stop to our house, walking behind her. It's not normal, is it?

But, Ruth spoke up. My father came home from work, with the same bluster as usual. He came down the stairs into the kitchen and not a word to Ruth. He sat down and grunted. Mother was in panic mode again. He was there and Ruth was there. Well, halfway through the meal I was thinking, *What do I say?* He just wouldn't speak to me. But

Ruth spoke to him. She turned around and said, 'Mr Maddocks, you are the rudest and most ignorant man I've ever had the misfortune to meet, and how you've got a son like Robert is beyond my comprehension.'

And she put down her knife and fork, got up and she walked out. Well, I jumped up and followed her up the road calling, 'Ruth, Ruth… I'm sorry.'

She said, 'Sorry? What for? I'll see you tomorrow.'

And that's the girl I married, and it's been sixty years.

We rented the house in St. Augustine's Road. It was a three bedroom house on a hill. I used to take the rent up on a Friday to a Mrs Davies at Grove Terrace. I went in there once, and a lady in her seventies, said to me, 'Robert, tell your father I'm giving up the house. The rent's going to be increased to £1 a week. Then I'm going to sell the house. Tell your father he can have the house for £500.'

After work I had to approach him with this information. I told him Mrs Davies was retiring and was going to sell the house, and he said, 'So what?' Well, I was trying to be polite and manly, but I was still a kid, wasn't I? I told him she would sell the house to him for£500. It was a three-bedroom house, overlooking the marina and I thought it was a good idea. I told him this, explaining how Mum would have her own home and we could do up the kitchen. I was quite handy with my hands. He said, 'When I want your advice, I'll ask for it. And I don't want this millstone around my neck for the rest of my life.'

I didn't understand that, but I had to go back and tell Mrs Davies that he wasn't interested. We didn't buy it. She sold it and we had to move out. He could have bought the house. He was a good decorator. As the years have gone by, I've kept a check on that house. It's sold about fifteen times, since 1952. The last price was £259,000. But we ended up in a council house at 81 Tennyson Rd.

I could have married other girls. My girlfriend next door,

Jennifer, was my playmate for years. They lived at 17 and we lived at 15. Her brother was called Robert Curren, Bobby, and there was another brother called Arthur Curren. So, Bobby was a good friend of mine. He couldn't read or write, but what a brain. He went into the scrap metal trade. We all ran around a lot and camped out together. And Jennifer was great too.

Dare, Truth, Kiss and Promises was a game we used to play. We had a lot of fun. We'd all lined up, the girls and the boys, Jennifer and Bobby and me and other kids, and the game would get to a point where you had to 'dare, truth, kiss or promise'. Bloody hell! We were kids. I guess about fourteen. We would dare each other to kiss this girl or that girl. It was all silly things. Anyway, this boy, another kid, was asked, 'Is it true, you love Jennifer?'

And the rules of the game meant that he had to tell the truth. 'Yes, I do,' he replied.

Then they dared him to kiss Jennifer.

'You come near me, I'll smash your face in,' she said.

Dare, truth, kiss and promises. We took it in turns. I have to be careful what I say here.

The local cinema was called The Washington. You'd go there to watch the local film and Jennifer worked there. She would be at the desk, taking the money. She'd then go around the corner, open the door, take back the ticket she'd just given me, get the flashlight out, and show me to my seat at the bottom. I remember a group of kids always being there, and she would shout at them to sit down.

Halfway through the film, Jennifer would pop up again with the ice cream tray. I never had much money and didn't usually have an ice cream, but I do remember a filthy dirty kid who sat next to me once. I forget his name now, but do remember feeling sorry for him. He approached Ruth for an ice cream and she said, 'Take your hand off that!' and smacked his hand.

*

We didn't go very far camping, just on what was called the Triangle, quite near our homes. We had a slight romance going on there. We went camping, but nothing ever happened. Despite this, when I first wanted to start courting Ruth, she said I was spoken for, thinking I was still with Jennifer. I was, kind of, but we were just kids, playmates really.

When Jennifer was older, she met a boy called Stan. We'd known him when we were younger and back then she'd said to me, 'Christ... he's bloody boring.' He worked in Howells in Cardiff and he used to sell carpets. One time we went into the arcade where he was selling the carpets. I can see it now: He was trying to sell a carpet to this lady. I remember Jennifer had her face pressed against the window. He was trying not to look at us. Anyway, 'Stan, Stan the Carpet Man' married her anyway and I'll tell you what, it was all good. She married well.

After Bobby died, I saw her and her children. They were all academics, speaking French, lovely girls. I think sometimes, she could have been my wife. We had a joke about it, saying I was her ex, but her daughters didn't know me at all. They'd no idea how close we had been. Life goes on... Bobby's dead... Jennifer is still alive. She's aged very rapidly, but life's hard work, isn't it?

I must tell this story, about Arthur and the Round Table...

Well, Arthur worked for the Gas Board and his job was to turn street gas lamps on and off. He did this at night and early in the morning. That was all he did, but he had a pike – a big long lance, and as he was called Arthur and, Bobby's first name was Lance. I put Arthur and the Lance together and called him Sir Launcelot. Everyone laughed, but Robert came down and asked me about it. He's dead now, died last year. Anyway, he asked me what all this Sir Launcelot stuff was about, and then told me not to mention it again. It had upset him, and he was plenty aggressive too. I said, 'Lance is a nice name.'

He stated, 'If you say it again I'll kill you.' And he meant it! He was very sensitive and he couldn't read or write. He went to sea, at the same time I did, but he went the wrong way. He joined the Norwegian fleet because his eyesight was bad. Now, they go up north, where it's cold. I went to the Caribbean and came back all bronzed and suntanned, but he only did one trip. 'Sod that,' he said, packing it in straight away. He went into scrap and made a fortune.

Around the corner from us were two people called Mrs Lock and Mrs Key. They both called their sons Ivor. Ivor was a great name in those days. There was Ivor Cullen, Ivor Lock and Ivor Key. I couldn't understand why you would call your son Ivor if your name was Lock or Key. They worked in scrap as well. I was always taking my father's scrap around to them in the evenings after school to sell. He got it from the docks, you see. They weighed it and I'd take the money down. It was always cash. Ivor Lock and Ivor Key lived next door to each other! You couldn't make it up, could you? Ivor Lock, Ivor Key. We had some fun with that. I'm not making it up!

There were other strange Welsh names as well, like Dai Death. Well, you can't get away with it now. He used to say, 'Don't let me down, boys.' So they called him Dai Balloon. Our two other neighbours were a husband and wife called Lyn and Jim, Mr & Mrs Lawe. So we called them 'jimlawelynlawe'. We'd say it over and over and it made us laugh.

There was another chap with a glass eye. We were fascinated by him. Of course, the poor man lost his eye in the war, didn't he? But as a kid, you'd zero in on the eye. He didn't have a patch, so you could see the glass eye, although we were told not to mention it.

Anyway, school days carried on. I did the Cubs and Boy Scouts and all that nonsense. But, as I mentioned previously, I was good at sport. On Sports Day once, they said there was a five-mile run. It was down to the headland, along the beach and back all the way up. But before going I had to go to the toilet and when I came out they'd gone, the entire school had gone.

A teacher said, 'You've got to get going, Maddocks.'

I said, 'Okay, sir.'

I shot off and I was passing everybody, about thirty or forty ahead of me. I passed them one by one and I was getting out of breath. But I was running so fast I was overtaking them. I came to the last bit of the run, back to the school and there were five in front of me. A boy called Wallace caught up with me and asked me where I'd been. He then said we had to sprint.

I said, 'What do you mean, sprint?'

I sprinted. I can't explain what happened next, but I sort of floated. Sebastian Coe had the same thing. I shot down there so fast, I nearly came in, but I couldn't pass the first bloke, who'd had that half mile start. I got to the end and I stopped. I saw Mr Ellis and I went 'hah!' Then I saw all the others breathing heavily. I thought, *Are you all right?* I hadn't realised I was able to recover so well.

Then there was javelin throw on Sport's Day.

'Up you get, Maddocks. You're on.'

I threw the javelin so far they said it had gone into the tree across the road. Of course, that led to them all talking, saying this bloke must be good.

Anyway, 1956 was a big year for me. To cut a long story short, there was a teacher. I think he's dead now, and his name was Mr Parry. He was an ex-military man. He was called Pasha Parry. He was a massive bloke. He taught history, which I did like, but I talked in class.

He came up to me and yanked me up. I was just a kid

and the same height as him, but he was massive. I was a bad pupil and he hit me, so hard. It's unbelievable. It took me over the table. I got up. I'd never been hit by anybody. I stood there for about five minutes, and the rest of the class froze. He told me to sit down and I said I preferred to stay standing. I was very polite. I said, 'With respect, I'll stand, sir.'

I stood there for three quarters of an hour. Then we all started to go out. I went straight past him. Next door was Mr Ellis. They were in adjoining classrooms. I went past him and he said he'd see me tomorrow. I said, 'I shan't be back tomorrow.'

He looked horrified, as I was top in French. But I never went back. We all accepted that you got smacked and got the cane, but I'd been thumped by a teacher. I was too ashamed and didn't think I could face him or the class.

Years later, I was in the Antiques Centre in Cardiff. A chap was there in his seventies and he started talking to me about it. He knew Mr Parry and said he'd recently been talking to him about what he'd done, and Mr Parry said that he sorely regretted it. I would have liked to meet him, but he died. But at least I knew that he regretted it.

And, I suppose, his actions set me on another path in life...

Chapter Four
All at Sea

I didn't exactly run away to sea. I went home, explained what had happened, and said that I wasn't going back to school. My next door neighbour, Bobby Curren was talking about going to sea, so I decided to follow.

I went to the sea training school in Cardiff, passed all the tests, and got through all the necessary nonsense: compass use, knots and sailing – anything you needed to know about shipping before you got on a boat. They taught you how to sail with the winds, how to tack, how to row, feather the oars and so on. It was all fun. It lasted about thirteen weeks and was good for me, and it got me out of being a student. I used to cycle there, back and forth from Penarth.

After the training, I walked in to the Shipping Federation in Mount Stuart Square and more-or-less announced that I wanted to join the Merchant Navy. I was a free spirit. I didn't have a girlfriend then. Of course, I thought about my mother, who was disappointed that I'd come out of grammar school. She didn't want me to go away to sea, but she wasn't going to stop me.

They give you the name of a ship. It can be any ship, but you don't have a choice. They told me to report to ship named Temple Inn in Alexander Docks, Cardiff. It was from London and it was going to Vancouver, Canada.

I had all my new gear and I had to walk through town to get to the ship. As I approached I thought, *Jesus, it's big. Very big. I can't do this.* But I plucked up the courage and I got on deck. It was bedlam.

'What the fuck do you want?' said a man.

I was only a kid. I replied. 'I'm reporting as a deck hand, sir.'

'Don't call me sir. You are a Peggy.'

'What's that?' I asked.

'The lowest on this bloody ship.'

His language was unbelievable. 'This is a fucking ship,' he said. 'You think you're educated?'

'No, sir,' I replied. 'I'm just reporting for duty and all I want to know is what I've got to do?'

'Find yourself a cabin astern, stow your gear,' he said.

So I did that. I put some working clothes on and went back up on deck to see what to do. There wasn't anyone there to ask. Then the bosun came along. He called me Ronnie. I asked what he wanted of me. He said the ship would sail in about four hours, that provisions were coming on board, and that we were loading cars, Jaguars. After that we'd be going to Fowey to load China clay, then into dry dock in Avonmouth for about two weeks. He told me all this and I wondered why they hadn't got me to join two weeks later.

But anyway, the crew started coming on board, the other deck hands. They were all in their thirties.

'Ronnie,' the bosun said. 'What you've got to do now is… we have to get steam on deck for the derricks and get ropes and wires in. Go down and see the chief engineer amid-ships and ask him for steam on deck.'

I didn't know at the time what that meant, so I went down the stairs. It was an unbelievable place, like Dante's Inferno – the noise, the bedlam… people running all about. So I politely asked, amongst all the f-words going on.

'The bosun wants steam on deck. I need to speak to the

chief engineer,' I said.

'Who do you think you are? The chief is down there, if you dare...'

I approached this guy and he exploded. I kind of realised what was going on then. He said they'd already got steam on deck and I realised I was being used. They just wanted to get rid of me. So I go back on deck and saw the bosun. He looked at me and asked if I was all right and I said yes.

'Lesson number one,' he said.

The ship didn't just sail off to Canada. It had to be provisioned. Soon it went to Fowey for the china clay and that's another story. I went ashore there. I had no money, but they took me into this so-called pub, where they served scrumpy cider. I don't remember the rest, but I woke up later at sea, sick as a dog.

In Fowey we loaded all the china clay. It was white stuff and it got everywhere, everything was white. We then headed for the dry-dock in Avonmouth. It was going to be there for two weeks, so the bosun said to me that I could go back home, if I wanted, with a rail warrant. Well, a week before I'd been in The Albion hotel, chatting to a bloke called Malcolm Salter, sitting on a bench close to the window, and I'd told him I was going to Vancouver. Well, of course, when I came back home on the train for that fortnight, I went down The Albion again. I shouldn't really have been in the pub, but there he was saying:

'I thought you were going to Vancouver.'

'I am,' I replied.

'You said that last time.'

I just nodded and took a sip of my drink.

Eventually, the ship did set off to Vancouver, but we had to go all the way down the Atlantic coast, right down to Panama. It was a long way and I was surprised how time flew by. The ship was just pounding along. By the time we got to Panama, I'd been trying to steer the ship and had been told off by the officers. The ship's routine involved watches and bell ringing, steering the ship, painting the ship, and night watch.

About a month out, I was steering the ship somewhere in the middle of the Atlantic and the second officer on the bridge – above the steering area – said that I needed to look ahead, to watch where I was going. He took me to the stern of the ship and was just winding me up a bit, saying I could use Iron Mike, which was their name for the automatic steering on the ship. Anyway, after a while, he got to know me well.

'What are you doing on this bloody ship?' he asked.

'I don't really know,' I replied. 'I'm just a kid going to Canada.'

'You know, some of the cadets are bloody idiots,' he said. 'You are way ahead of them. You should do some proper training at Smith's Nautical College.'

'I can't do maths,' I replied. I didn't really want to be at sea all my life anyway.

He moved me from the stern, where I looked after the crew, doing all their food and put me amidships with the cadets. Well, they were upset about that. The deck crew were furious, so I had to go back. It nearly caused a bloody mutiny.

After a long, long time, we eventually arrived in Vancouver. Before I left Cardiff I had to learn about the routine of ringing bells at night. If you see lights: three bells for dead-ahead, one bell for starboard and two for port. It only works at sea though, and I was on the coast at Cardiff, ringing bells for ages.

Vancouver was amazing. I felt so privileged to be a foreign port at that age, just sixteen. Probably too young. I was just a kid. I hadn't even started shaving yet. I didn't consider my sister and parents who might have worried about me. You don't when you're a kid. To me, the thing was such an adventure and I was getting £4 a week. It was full board of course, because you can't get off the ship. I was sending postcards back to my grandparents. I've still got those at home. I wrote it all down… *'Dear Grandad, we're going through the Panama Canal now.'*

On that ship, I was the lowest of the low, but there was also a chap called George from Grangetown, Cardiff. He wanted to write a letter to his wife, Mabel. He wanted to say that we'd arrived in Panama, but he couldn't write. He asked me to do it for him. He was very polite, but I was embarrassed. I read it back to him and he said he'd sign it, but he just put a cross. He was an able-bodied seaman. You'd entrust your life to him on the ship and you feel more protected after that.

I got beaten up by two E.D.H deck-hands, but that's another story. They didn't like me. I beat them up too, but that's also another story. Often on board you have to be on your guard. In particular, it was obvious that the Arabs didn't like us. One I called Abdul. It wasn't his name, but that's what we called him. He was splicing some wire in the turrets and something happened. A marlin spike fell from my hand and hit him on his toe. It was the blunt end, thank goodness, but he was wearing sandals. He cursed at me. The ship was rolling around, but he didn't stop.

'I'll kill you, I'll kill you. I'll kill you,' he said.

I remember it. He picked up the spike and came after me and struck at me, and a spark came off the side of the masthead. It was a big mast. I ran around it and out of the room, out onto the deck. I was on the port side. He was running after me, shouting unbelievable things. I was just sixteen.

He said, 'All your women are whores.' That's what he said to me.

I thought, *Fuck this.* I stopped and turned around and came up beside the boson. He was looking at me, so I ran the other way. But his words angered me and I turned on him. He fled down the hold, grabbing the iron rungs that went down the side. That wasn't a safe escape though and he quickly realised he'd nowhere to go.

I shouted to him, 'You'll meet your maker now.' And he started to cry. I thought, *What am I doing?*

It's a long way down into the hold. I calmed him down. I grabbed him and pulled him back on deck and I never had a problem with him again. I don't know why he ranted on at me.

We had all sorts on that ship: Maltese, who openly carried knives, and Somalis. I was surprised I survived the trip. Anyway, we got to Vancouver. The ship had to moor up to load some more timber. I went ashore in the early evening, about half past three or four. The bosun gave me a couple of dollars and said, 'Ronnie, be back by five.' I went into town, a lovely town it was. I took in a baseball game. I don't know why I did that. It was just more exciting. I was lost really, like a kid in a candy store. Of course, I came back late. I don't remember how late. The harbour was vast and the ship, Temple Inn was big, almost 10,000 tons. But, it had gone. The ship was not there.

I spoke to a chap with a cap on, a ship's master, I think he was.

'Sir… The Temple Inn… It's not there,' I asked him politely.

'What do you mean, not there? It's been moved upstream. Look at you, idiot. Did you think the captain would be coming into town to look for you and where you are?'

I asked what I should do and he suggested I should start walking upstream, but it's not just as a simple as 'upstream'. It was a vast area. There were loads of trees going down to the river and it was getting dark, but I thought I'd better get going. I was stuck in a foreign country with no money. I'd spent my bloody money. I followed the river and I eventually found the ship. I must admit it was quite a relief. The ship was working with a skeleton crew, loading timber.

It was all Douglas fir timber, coming back to Britain and it was bedlam on there. I wasn't involved, but I was terrified.

'Heh, Ronnie, you won't be late again, will you?' the bosun asked.

'No,' I replied.

'See, you learn, don't you… you learn, rapidly!' he said.

Anyway, by the time they'd finished up, half the crew had disappeared. They had joined another ship, for another country. So we were short on crew. The Stevedores used to chat me up, asking why I didn't jump ship. But I couldn't do that. I was just a kid of sixteen. If I'd done that my whole life would have changed.

It took a long time to get back, but we did eventually get back to Cardiff. And we got paid off. It was a big day that was. You've been on a ship for so long, so when you come off you have what they call 'seaman's roll'. This is when you stand on solid ground. It's weird. It's hard to explain, unless you've been to sea. It feels like a whole new environment.

I then went ashore and got paid off. The two deck hands that had beaten me up shared a taxi with me into town. I remember one was called Vince and he did get his comeuppance. Let me take you back…

When you join a ship for the first time, you have to have all the gear. I'd had to buy sea boots, socks, a Sou'Wester and so on, and, in those days, you had a duffel bag. After the bosun had sent me to stow my gear I found myself in a cabin on the port side. There were a few other first timers and two EDH: efficient deck hands they were called. Both were from Cardiff, John and Vince; thirty year olds, hardened and experienced. Well, I guess they saw me as a target, with all this new gear.

After being at sea for a while, and completing various jobs on deck, I went back to my cabin. I shared it with a guy called Derek Powell and he had the top bunk. I was on the bottom. Anyway, I went to sleep. I woke up and I was pinned, completely pinned down by something. I couldn't move and I was being pummelled. At first I thought I was having a bad dream, but it was them. They took my pocket watch. It wasn't worth much, but it gave me the time. They left me in a right state. I eventually went back up on deck and they thought it was hilarious. They almost wet themselves. But, as you can imagine, I was pretty angry. I had no idea why they'd done it. I'd just been pummelled for no reason. I hadn't done anything to provoke it. They just didn't like me. I'd had a few arguments with people before that, but nothing like this.

The bosun saw me and asked if I was all right. I said I'd had an accident, but he knew. He told me to keep my cool and reminded me we still had a long voyage to complete. After that, I did get friendlier with some of the other more experienced seamen, the ABs. This made me feel I had a bit more control of things. I did have a go at the two of them on the deck one day. I reminded them we would be on the ship for a few months and said, 'Every day, look over your shoulder.'

I told them I wanted my watch back before we got off the ship. I did get it back, but they held onto it for quite a length of time. They'd taken one of my jerseys too, literally stealing the shirt off my back. The bosun knew what was going on, up to a point. There was no use complaining to him and I knew those two were older and wiser than me.

Anyway, we got back into Cardiff docks and got paid off. I went right up to their face and asked if they wanted to share a taxi. They said they would. I wanted to see where they were living. As it happened though, they dropped me off first and carried on. I had another go at them though. My words were pretty sharp, but again I told them to keep looking over their shoulders. They told me to f-off and off they went.

I got a nice homecoming from my mother. It was late in 1956. After that, nothing happened for about two months, but soon after I told mates about them. One of them, an Irishman called Pat Woolahan suggested we should sort them out. He's dead now, poor bugger. He was a bit of a thug and fast with his fists, but a good mate to me. He said they were just bullies and it happened all the time, but I was still angry and I wasn't going to let those two forget it.

So, eventually, one day we happened to be in a pub, off Newport Rd. It was a popular pub for seamen. Vince and John had mentioned it and I'd remembered it all. I didn't think on it every night, but one evening we parked up there and went in. I was standing at the bar with my mate and I saw one of them. I'm sure it was Vince. I was a little agog and my mate asked me if I was okay. I explained that I'd just seen one of the blokes in the pub that had beaten me up on the ship.

'Right then,' he said. 'Are we going to have a go?'

'No,' I replied. 'Stay there.'

I put my glass down. It was probably a Guinness. The bar was crowded and it felt like there was a mist hanging in the air. I walked over and he saw me coming. He turned to stand up from his stool. I hit him. Just hit him, as hard as I could. He fell back and broke the window and then he ran out. No one in the pub moved. It was a working man's pub. Today, it would cause a bloody riot. But, that was it.

Pat said to me, 'Christ, Ronnie… you've changed.'

I said I was still the same bloke, but that I just hadn't needed his help. Anyway, Vince ran off, hopefully instilled with the fear now that I'd be behind him all the time! But, I was satisfied, and I didn't come across Vince or John on any other ship, and usually I was quite a popular guy with the older hands.

In those days a telegram boy would come to the house. It sounds very basic now, but that's how it was. I got a telegram at home from The Shipping Federation in Mount Stuart Square. The Federation were the people who effectively employed me, and told me which ships to go on. I used to know his name, the officer in charge. He was a very nice man. They always needed seamen, so they'd have a look around to work out who was already at sea, and who was at home, and then they'll send a telegram. The telegram told me to go to Cardiff Docks to pick up a new ship, the Baron Renfrew to go to West Africa. That ship was owned by the Hogarths in Glasgow. People called them the Hungry Hogarths because food was always so tight. It didn't cause a mutiny, but off the coast of West Africa it was a bit like that, because the crew wanted more food. We got more food, but those old Hogarths were horrible things, almost scrap they were, rusty tin cans.

Of course, I had to join it. That was my job. Mind you, there was a pub on the Cardiff docks that everyone got drunk in before joining a ship. You sort of had to. The Federation gave you an allowance, a sort of advance on your salary, four or five pounds. So you'd go in the pub and drink that. Some would come out the pub and jump ship there and then, the 'Pierhead Jump' it was called. Of course, this is all history now, but when you're young, you don't think life will change that much. It's all completely gone now. If I go back to Cardiff today, I can't recognise any of it. All the pubs have gone. It's all posh houses now, it's not the same. So much has changed in my time, and not for the better. We used to know all the people's homes, their addresses and their families, and people were courteous and polite. Nowadays it's just money, money, money – it's unbelievable!

Anyway, I'd gone up in the ranks now. I was not basic anymore. I was a junior ordinary seaman and the next rank would have been ADH (Advanced Deckhand), but I only got up to JOS (Junior Ordinary Seaman). You're still learning the trade, how to run a ship, and you still have to do what you are bloody told.

It was a new crew, all different people, and this time I

could feel a changed atmosphere on the ship. The crew were all rubbish, a bit like me, but also they were all rough types. The bosun wasn't interested in me. We moved off with all the usual clamour, noise and bedlam, headed for Conakry and Freetown in West Africa.

The ship wasn't well run and halfway across the Atlantic the chap in charge of the crew announced that he was going to go and see the captain. We wanted more food. It was a bit like *Mutiny on the Bounty*. I was still a kid, having an adventure, so I just went along with it. I was hungry, but they were all older than me. They decided to put down their tools and stop working, unless they got more food. We were given rations like it was the Victorian days. The ship was run on a shoestring and it was dangerous, the rust was unbelievable. You daren't try and shift it. It would just have crumbled, leaving a hole.

When we got to West Africa the first time, the ship went up to the harbour. In truth, it wasn't really a harbour, just a river with tree trunks – very basic. I watched the people loading the ship. We were taking iron ore from West Africa, back to Port Talbot. I watched these people, going up and down the gangplank, with these baskets of iron ore. I was thinking, *God help us*. Life was so much easier for people with cranes back in Port Talbot. Anyway, we were docked for about a week.

They were French speakers there and, of course, I had to try my French out on shore. The so-called old sea dogs wanted me up there, and said I should chat up the women for them. Well, I got it all wrong. I don't know if I got the gender wrong, but I got it all wrong.

It was Freetown in Sierra Leone and things were pretty basic there. With the ship moored and tied up, we were told pretty firmly to keep the portholes shut. But, when I went ashore, I left my porthole open. I had wanted some air to get in. When the tide comes in and the ship rises, the porthole became quite level with the quay. When I got back to the ship, they'd stolen all my bed sheets. All my sheets had gone. I had to pay for that. Another fine. I learned not to leave the porthole open!

But anyway, I went into town with the crew. They were really rough. Actually beyond rough. There were about twelve of them. They were all over me, all the old sea dogs. They didn't give a monkeys. All they wanted was to have a good time in any pub they could find, and to find women. At sixteen or seventeen years old, I wasn't really interested, but they used me because I had some knowledge of French. This was pretty weird. For a young lad of sixteen to try and chat up women in French in their fifties. But the crew were using me as a kind of a lure, and in Britain I still wouldn't have been allowed in the pubs. Out there, they weren't exactly pubs though.

What happened is a bit of a blur, as after a few pints of that crazy drink they had out there, I was in a world of my own. But somehow I must have said something wrong and I insulted the local women who called the police. They turned up in their vans, speaking English and they arrested the entire crew and put us on a traffic island, with more police around us. It was unbelievable, but I can't recall it all. The crew were all drunk of course. I wasn't so much, but I'd had a few too many. I wondered what was going to happen next.

Well, the captain turned up. He had been called to pay a ransom, or a fine, and was mad as hell. He spoke to the policeman in charge, then came over and spoke to the bosun, accusing the others of 'leading this young boy astray', meaning me. There I was, looking all innocent, but the others said that I'd caused it all. He asked if I'd been speaking in French and I tried to explain that it was schoolboy French and I didn't know all the right genders, etc. Anyway he paid the fine to release us from the traffic island, and we went back to the ship.

Well, the air was quite blue then. I got fined for losing my bedsheets from the cabin and they never let me forget about it. But it was a good day, and we got back safely. They loaded the ship and it was a pretty uneventful trip back. I had loads of hassle from people trying to put their stamp on my youth, and the language was always pretty volatile. It was necessary in this situation.

We arrived after about six weeks. In Cardiff, we finished the trip and got paid off, end of story. I got discharged, with my book stamped 'very good' and off I went.

The third ship I went on was called Ripon. A lovely ship she was. Also an iron ore carrier, but a much more modern ship; self-loading with big winches. It was modern and to me it was amazing. I went to Conakry again, and to Freetown. It had a very good crew and a very good captain. The ship ploughed on and there was no problem on that ship at all. I was learning a lot, but there was almost no maintenance whatsoever to do this time, because it was, as far as I could tell, a brand new ship. It was an uneventful trip on a lovely ship, with good food, cooked by a chef who came from Penarth, who knew me and looked after me. He was called Johnny Fish or Roger Fish, I forget the first name. We used to call him Fish anyway.

We went back to the same ports, but although I was a bit worried about it, I had no problems this time going ashore. The second officer did ask me, as I'd been asked before, what on earth I was doing working on a ship. All I could reply was that I was there to learn about working in the Merchant Navy. We got back, signed off again in Cardiff. We're into 1957 now.

There's a lot of routine on a ship and of course it's moving all the time. They had a saying: 'Don't pee against the wind.' I remember that one. But I didn't really like being at sea. I missed the home comforts. I was thinking it was a crazy life I'd got into, but I had seen a bit of the world. It had been roughly two years at sea. Actually maybe not as long as that. Perhaps a year and a half during '56 and '57. Anyway, it seems a long time when you're on a ship.

In did try working on a coaster called Pirell, thinking I'd be home most nights. I'd gone into the office in Mount Stuart Square and asked if I could go on a coaster for a while. He advised me not too, saying they were filthy, dirty workhorses. I didn't take his advice and joined a ship in Barry Docks. It was a tramp-steamer, a horrible little thing. I went on-board and the first thing I noticed was the filth and dirt. The cabin I had was so close to the deck head that my face was touching the top, covered in rust and dripping with salt water.

It was so cold too. The ship went on a trip along the south coast somewhere, but I didn't stay. I lasted about a week. I gave up, went home and decided that was the end of my sea going career. It wasn't my thing; I wasn't happy. I thought I'd get back on dry land, enjoy some nights out, wear some decent clothes and have a good time. So that was the end of that.

Obviously, it had been interesting and it was a good experience, that's the thing.

Chapter Five
Wanderlust Years

1958 – 1976

'We were all the same weren't we, in those days: always looking to see where we could find a place in life, where we might go."

I was now ashore for good and I had to find work. My mother wasn't very pleased. My father wasn't really interested. All he said to me was, 'You'd better get a job. I'm not going to support you, while you're lying on your back.'

I felt I had to do something. I was supposed to be educated and I had been drifting around too much. While my father worked in Cardiff docks, I was still looking for work. With all the men at work (unless you were dying or ill, of course), I felt so out of place. Later, when I had a broken leg from a fall at work, I got accosted on the street in Penarth. A woman asked me why I wasn't working. It was obvious why. I was limping and in a plaster. Despite this, she had no sympathy for me, saying that I should just get on with it, and that all men should be working.

I first went to work at Currans in Cardiff. I was there for about a year. Currans was in Grangetown. It was a massive factory that employed everybody. It did everything, from making armaments in the war, to pots and pans and general haberdashery. It's all gone now. But, during that time, I used to travel from Penarth for about three or four miles to Cardiff. I used to run to work, unbelievably. I can't even believe it now. I used to run from Penarth, through the tunnel and up into Cardiff; work all day and run back home. I can't imagine it now, and how stupid it was. I was so fit and I had the energy to burn. The tunnel is also gone. It used to run under the river Ely, from Penarth to Grangetown in Cardiff. We used to run through the tunnel when we were kids, and even more so when I had a motorbike.

Here's an interesting story. Currans employed hundreds of people. I was a paint sprayer for a while. In another part of the factory they employed all the girls from Cardiff and one of them was Shirley Bassey. She worked on the pots and pans section, putting the enamel on bowls. I remember all the girls sitting in a line, but I didn't know who they were. They were all black girls. I was a seventeen-year-old boy, pushing a big trolley full of beds past all these girls. I used to get ripped to pieces, but as time went on and on, I got chattier and started shouting back. They loved that! I won't tell you what they used to shout. It was often quite offensive, and sexual at times.

We got talking one night after work and decided to go up to the pub in Tiger Bay. It was on James Street. There was a boxer called Joe Erskine and he was the landlord at The Loudoun. We used to go there for a drink, with two girls: Shirley and a girl called Omo. She was called Omo because there was a washing powder in those days with the tagline, 'Omo washes whiter'. We'd have half a glass of lager, or whatever, and go home. There was nothing sexual, we were just kids.

Shirley used to go into the pubs and sing. Okay, you know who she is today and where she's come from, but for me then it was just entertainment. She was told not to sing in the pubs by these bloody idiots, but there you are. When

Shirley Bassey went overseas, she didn't have any self-conscious thoughts about being black, but she suffered segregation, even in the swimming pools. It's sad isn't it: she was just another girl to us. People coming to the UK from the West Indies didn't have any negative impact on our lives. We had a shortage of workers such as bus drivers. It was mainly Jamaica they came from. We lived with them, in pubs and clubs and so forth. I've been to places around the world, and you just have to blend in. I'm very good at doing this. I was shy, but people seemed to like me and I just got on with it.

I will tell you an embarrassing story from my youth. I've never mentioned this to anybody. It happened when I was maybe eighteen or nineteen. I would often meet a girl from work and go out to the picture house with her in Cardiff. The Capitol in Queen Street it was called. One day, I went to see a film with a young girl in tow. You'd sit in the back row and I think *Ben Hur* was on, or some monster thing. I wasn't really interested in the film, of course. There was nothing especially amorous going on, just holding hands.

I had to go to the toilet. Now, you've got to go past a lot of people if you are in the middle of the bloody row. So I struggled to get out. The toilet was on the right hand side, just under the stage. Well, I went and I did my wee and as I zipped up I caught the loose skin of my penis. The zip wouldn't move. It was jammed there and I was in agony. I wasn't quite screaming, but I was seeing blood. I could hear *Ben Hur* in the background and the roar of the crowd. I was in there a long, long time, struggling with the zip. If I moved it down it hurt; if I moved it up it hurt. I'd been in there about fifteen minutes and thought, *I've got to do something serious now or that girl will have disappeared.* I had to go down with the zip quickly. I did and the pain was enormous. I got a load of paper and stuffed it down my trousers and crept back into the auditorium. In my head I thought that everyone would suspect what had been going on. Well, there was no girl there. She'd gone. I wasn't really interested in any amorous connection there and then. I struggled back to the seat and had to watch the whole film in a lot of pain. It does happen. It's a true story and I've only ever told it once in my life – now, today.

I didn't last long at Currans. I soon decided to move on. So I left. My mother was not impressed with my moving about, but we were living in another house then in Tennyson Road. These people came to stay with us, who were working on the docks. They were building a new pier on Penarth Docks. It was to be a four-bay pier with concrete pontoons. These workers came from a company in London called G Tate & Co. Civil Engineers. They came to stay in our house for Bed & Breakfast. One worker was called Tom and the other Harry. Tom was the foreman. He was sixty-five, very Cockney, but a nice chap. He asked me if I was looking for work. I said I was, and he invited me down to join them.

We walked down to the docks from our house every morning to work on this jetty. It's still there today. I was working on that at the docks at Penarth for two years between '58 and '60. The jetty goes out into what was the channel, which had a forty-two-foot drop; the second-highest tide in the world, roughly. It's quite a bit. The other one is in New York.

Well, where the tide goes in and out, they built this pier and, as I say, it's still there. My granddaughter went down to take a picture of it and she was impressed. It's the one I built. Well, strictly the one that I worked on. It was interesting work and it was good money, but that's when I injured my leg. I tripped over a bit of wood and fell forty feet – that's a long way to go. I couldn't move for about an hour, as I guess I had a trapped nerve. Anyway, I was forty feet down, lying on these timbers, thinking, *This is the end of me*. The tide was coming in too. Tom was stressing out. He was worried about what my mother might say. Her son was lying there injured.

It was my fault and, anyway, the crane driver George came along, trundling along the tracks. He lowered his hook down and they tied me on a stretcher. It's unbelievable now, but they lifted me up and set me on the docks. It was so embarrassing. I was conscious while all this was going on. They were telling me I was all right and not to worry. They sent for the medics. I got in the ambulance and went off to Cardiff. They soon sorted my leg out, and had a week off work. As I mentioned, that's when I got told off for walking around the streets of Penarth during the working day.

As they used to say on the ships: one hand for self, one hand for the ship. This was my lesson to 'always look down and make sure you don't trip over anything!'

A few weeks later I got back to work and stayed there two years. It was a good job and I was very popular. I actually moved with the company when they undertook projects in Port Talbot and up to London. It was very interesting work. Heavy work, but good money and I learned a lot.

It was while I was working on the jetty at Penarth docks that I met Keith Loughborough. Across from the docks was a little shop. It's gone now, of course. Well one day, about a year before, Keith's mother, who owned the shop, walked across the lock gates and fell in. Her leg got crushed between the gates. It was my father who yanked her out. He pulled her out and gave her first aid. She lost her leg, but she did get a big payout after the accident. With this money, she bought the shop and Keith a car. I used to go across to the shop to buy cigarettes for all the men and got chatting with Keith. I didn't smoke, never have, but I was sent over for the others and I got sweets and chocolate.

Every Saturday Keith and I would go to the pub and the dancehall. It was on one of these nights out that I met my girlfriend, Ruth. She wasn't impressed at first, but in time, we got together. Her mother was initially not interested in me... oh, no. An ex-seaman and ex-labourer, definitely not!

At the time, Ruth was courting Tony Coulthard (only because he did her maths homework for her). That's awfully bad, isn't it? That's how cruel women are! Well, in time I wore Mrs Chapman down and won her over.

One day, when I was working on the pier at Penarth, Ruth walked down the hill. She was with a friend, but it was obvious that she had come to see me. Well, imagine how embarrassing that was. I was with all my workmates, about twenty of them, all in their thirties. She was my girlfriend, so I would have normally been happy to see her, but not in those circumstances. They just took the mick out of me. Tom Southard, the foreman, who was in his sixties, suggested I take her in the big shed. There was a fire going there and I made her some tea. This just made it worse. I was with two girls in this big shed and I was trying to be relaxed. As soon as the girls left, Jesus Christ, they let me have it, and they never stopped. I was the youngster. They ripped me to death. I won't go into all the rudeness, but they were saying I'd got two girlfriends now and I'd be in trouble when they saw my mother. I knew they were winding me up, but imagine trying to explain yourself. I got wound up at first, but I ended up giving as good as I got, saying, 'I suppose you couldn't pull a few birds, could you, at your age.'

It was banter and it got you through the day. I remember them all. Alec Taylor was one, ex-Royal Navy and Roy Downs, another character. He used to chant ditties to me:

'Fire, fire,' said Mrs Dyer.
'Where, where,' said Mrs Bear.
'Down the docks,' said Mrs Cox.
'Any damage,' said Mrs Savage.
'None at all,' said Mrs Hall.

And he'd go on like that. Fancy that, I can repeat it now after all those years. He was an alcoholic, but a lovely guy. And there was Jackson; a forty-year-old mental case, who drove our Land Rover to get the pay on a Friday. He'd been in a mental home at some point. I knew that because he had told me. The crane driver was called John, an Irishman. They hauled Jackson up in the wooden toilet one day, strapped the door shut and had him swinging over the basin. He was pretty mad when they brought him back to land, but he had a certificate he used to show around that specifically said that he had been certified as sane. We used to wind him up terribly. They were a great crowd and they made a big mark in my life.

But I soon found out that Keith was a nasty piece of work. Ruth told me she didn't like him. He's dead now. But I met his wife, quite recently, in the Talbot pub. She asked if I'd known him. I said yes and she told me he had hated me, because I went into the police force. He was a criminal you see: stealing cars. They stayed together though for twenty years, so he must have had something about him. He was a charmer, that's what he was.

So, I worked with G. Tate & Co. until 1961, I think it was. Or, maybe I had a little while doing nothing in late 1960. But I had to impress this girl now. I had to get my act together. There was a company called Hancocks – a brewery in Cardiff, near the docks. It was not far down from Currans in Harper Street, I think. I applied to be a labourer there. They put me on a lorry one day as a driver's mate. I was fit. We drove all around the valleys, offloading barrels and I started learning about all the places they delivered to; getting to know everyone and how to fill in the sheets and all that. We would go in the pubs and I used to have an orange juice. I used to drink a pint of it, but the driver had beer. Each round was maybe about five drops; well that's five pints of beer, isn't it?

The pubs would give us free cigarettes. I didn't smoke, but I took them home, as they were free. I'd go back to the brewery and dole them out. I was like Father Christmas. They loved me. About a month later they offered me a job as a driver. I was old enough then, so I went in for their driving test and passed that. The next day they said, 'There's your lorry.'

It was a green lorry, a Bedford, and number seventeen. I remember the number. So I took that on and did that for about two years. Pretty much every pub you went in had some sort of problem. You were constantly trying to satisfy them all, but it was a great life, delivering barrels of beer. One guy in City Road once told me that he had hundreds of empty crates lying around because no one would take them back. I took as many as I could for him, but I had so many on the lorry it was bloody high and it was dangerous. I got stopped by the police, but of course they knew Hancocks and told me to get back to the brewery before the crates fell off. They were happy enough with that. Mind you, if the police had ever taken a breath test with some of those drivers! I didn't drink in those days, not when I was working. When you got back, you might have a Brains Dark. They had a cellar bar there. It was like a pub, but it was in a cellar. You'd go down there and they just give you a pint. No money. One pint I'd have, that's all, and then drive home. But some would stay there until the morning!

I remember going to a pub in The Hayes in Cardiff. It was stinking, it was. There were slops all over the place from the night before and ash trays full up.

'Christ sake, get this place cleaned up,' I said.

They said, 'Who are you?'

I'd maybe spoken a little too loudly you see. But it was disgusting. It was filthy. It's gone now. It was called The Cottage.

Another pub was in Queen Street. The traffic wardens used to come along, but they couldn't really say I couldn't park there, because I had to deliver the beer. They'd try and say I was causing an obstruction. I told them not to bother me, but to go in the pub and tell them they can't have their beer. So I got away with that. The police were quite good to me. I used to chat with them.

Hancocks still operated the old horse and dray too, with the rubber tyres in Cardiff. That was a sight to see that was… *clip clop, clip clop.* I also remember the trolley buses. It's a different world. Back then, I think people had more time for each other.

Pubs were just pubs in those days. I knew every pub in Cardiff, the Valleys and Penarth. It was very busy. I used to go to work in the mornings, load up and off I'd go. The day flew by. By now I had a heavy goods licence and a bit of experience behind me. I ended up with the Dinas Powys run and I stuck that until 1962. I did it quite well. I was developing physically, what with carrying all the barrels, and I had no problems at all, except that I got restless again.

Ruth's mother was pushing me a bit now too. I'd left the job at Hancocks and she asked me what I was going to do now. I replied that I didn't know. She said that if I wanted to get married to her daughter, I had to do something and, for some reason, she suggested that I apply to the police force. She knew that was a stable job, with a flat or a house. So I applied. That's life, you know. In those days we were always looking to see where we could find a place in life, where we might go.

Before the police I did another job with a small firm called FFAW. This was only for a short time, while I was waiting to join the force. There, I worked on a potato lorry. I had my dog with me then. Storm, his name was. I got him around 1961. Mr Adams was the owner at FFAW. I used to get the sacks of potatoes from Hereford and bring them back and deliver them. I remember I had to reverse up a very narrow lane in Porthcawl once. I did it, delivered the potatoes, and then walked the dog on the beach. I told Mr Adams I'd applied for the police, but he didn't seem to think I was very suitable for that. It was probably my first application, and Cardiff did turn me down.

Applying to join the Coventry City force wasn't prompted by anything, I just picked it and it was my last chance, too. If that hadn't worked I would have gone on the scrap.

Now, my mate Bobby Curren said, 'Don't go in the Cop Shop, please, Rob. Come and work with me on the scrap.'

I almost agreed thinking I didn't have anything else to do. But I felt I had to be responsible. I had a girlfriend and wanted to get married.

Bobby's father was called Ivor Curren and he'd always liked me, and Bobby liked my dad. I said we should swap, as Bobby liked the gardening and the fishing and that was more what my dad wanted. Now, Ivor Cullen, he was a mechanic and he had a garage. When I was working in Hancocks, Christmas time came and I had to get something, so Ivor said, 'Take the car.' It was an Alvis, with a big long bonnet on it. Bobby never got the keys off him, but I drove an Alvis into Cardiff, to Hancocks, for Christmas Eve. I didn't think about it then, but it was because he liked me, I think.

I hadn't really found what to do with myself. I've never really found what to do. My life has always been overtaken by… life itself. I didn't plan it. People do have quiet lives. People work in factories all their lives – they get a pension, they go home. I haven't.

You fall into things, or upon things, and it works out just right.

Chapter Six
Coventry City Police

So I joined the police force. This was an interesting time in my life. I joined in 1962 and left in 1966. Initially I was worried because I was so easy going. I was concerned that I might let them off, but, I must admit, it helped me come out of my shell.

My mother died in 1961. She never knew that I made it into the police force. She would have been very proud of me. When I was younger, she'd run the house like a bloody machine: cooking, washing and everything.

She got upset that I went to sea, but she was always there. She was very attractive and had always been slim, but then she started putting some weight on. Through the years, she was increasingly complaining about pains, and was in and out of the hospital. It was a long, drawn out affair, until we discovered that she had cancer that had spread right through her body.

My sister, Hilary, had to take over running the house, like an unpaid slave. She stopped going to school. We never really talked much about it then. She was also quite shy, although she married well. We were always close and later, when we would sit together, we did talk about it.

But, at the time, I didn't really know how ill my mother was. Hilary used to go and visit her in hospital and would come away, very upset. Looking back, we should have had more help. My father wasn't interested. He'd always just seen my mother as a workhorse. There was no love there. Sadly, my mother died in the hospital soon after.

One day, I was driving my father somewhere in the van. He said, 'I want no more talk about May.' This was strange and, as you can imagine, it made me angry.

She was cremated in Thornhill, Cardiff. It was a shame she passed away before I got into the police force.

At first, I got turned down by Cardiff, Glamorgan and the MET. Later, I discovered that when I applied to Cardiff, they spoke to my father. They went to my home to see my parents and my father told them to fuck off. If you're trying to get into the police and they visit your house and you are told to f-off, it doesn't do you a lot of good. When I applied to the MET police, I was very outspoken. Perhaps they saw me as a loose cannon, restless and unsettled, which was true.

But I had a lot of knowledge. Given my background, I was intelligent, had good sense and was practical, so I tried again.

I applied to Coventry and I went for the interview. I didn't like the look of Coventry when I got there. It had been bombed out in the war, of course. I quickly decided that if I didn't get in there I was going to join Bobby Curran in the scrap metal work. I went there, dressed in my best and stood in front of this bloke, the chief constable. He looked at me. He was standing to attention in front of me, but that's not my way.

'Young man,' he said. 'You've been turned down by Cardiff City Police.'

'Yes.'

'You've been turned down by Glamorgan County, Oh… and the MET. You've been written off. Why should I take you on as a police officer?'

Well, I came out of my shell then, and at that point, I wasn't that interested in staying.

'With respect, sir,' I said, 'my father is a blacksmith's striker—'

'…and you also left your grammar school,' he interrupted.

I didn't tell him I'd been beaten up. I just said I couldn't stand it.

'You're obviously not a settled young man, so why should I take you on in the Coventry City Police?'

So, I went on… 'Well, with respect, sir. Just look at what you've got in front of you and judge for yourself. Make a judgement on me.' I thought I was saying too much but I added, 'I can walk the job.'

'Pardon?' he asked.

'Walk the job. I will walk this job,' I replied.

He said he'd let me know.

A week later I got the letter telling me I'd been accepted as a police officer. It told me where to report to and gave me a date and time.

I couldn't believe I'd got in. I was twenty-two. Ruth was quite happy. So I headed off to Coventry, with Ruth staying behind in Cardiff. I was with my colleague: 401. Those were our numbers: 401 and 402. I forget his name. The police arranged a room for us. It was bed & breakfast. It was a simple arrangement, but unfortunately I had my dog with me. I forgot to mention this. They accepted the dog reluctantly, but we had to leave after a while, because the dog chewed up their garden.

It was an Alsatian called Storm. I got him when I was younger, before joining the police. At that time, I was still quite shy and thought it would be easier to meet people if I was walking a dog. A friend of mine, a hairdresser, had a dog called Mitzi. He told me he'd got it from someone in one of the back streets. They were a bit dodgy, but they were pedigree dogs. We went round to the place together. You wait to see which dog might come up to you, and this one did. He was small, just a puppy and wouldn't let go. I felt I couldn't walk out then. He cost me £10.

At that time, I was still living at 81 Tennyson Road, with my parents. My mother was still in hospital. I was living with my father and grandmother, who had moved in with us after my grandad passed away. It was a three-bed house, so not massive.

I put paper down in the bedroom for the dog. He was peeing all night and I had to clean it all up. He was only a puppy. It didn't take that long to train him. We bonded quite quickly. He'd bark, sit, stand, and walk to heel, do anything. He was a very clever, intelligent dog. I used to take him out in the lorry with me. I used to make deliveries to Porthcawl and he'd play on the sands there. Eventually, we had to put him to sleep, which was a kindness for him. I couldn't do it and funnily enough, Barbara, Ruth's sister, was the one who took him in.

First thing I did was go to a place called Ryton on Dunsmore, the training school, somewhere in Warwickshire. In 1962 it cost £75,000 to train a police officer. Interestingly this equalled the value of crimes I solved in my first year. I told the chief constable I'd paid for my training, but he didn't like being told. He was still happy though, having taken a chance on me.

I was at Ryton about three months, learning how to do the job. There were all sorts there: Cardiff policemen were there, asking me why I hadn't got in in Cardiff. I explained that I didn't know. The training school was interesting. You had to be trained to do all these jobs. Now, there's always someone that'll try and take advantage. One time we were being taught how to arrest somebody on an artificial layout. I was happy to play along. Well, one chap when I said, 'I was arresting him' actually started resisting me. I told him that when the roles were reversed I'd do the same to him, but suggested it might be better if he didn't resist. He continued to do so. I had no choice but to bosh him on the head. Well, you're not supposed to do that, but he was my age.

'What do you think you are playing at?' asked the chap in charge.

'I'm just play-acting,' I replied.

When you're trying to arrest someone who doesn't want to be arrested, you hit them with the truncheon in the right place, to neutralise their muscles. You don't hit them over the head! The words they used were 'minimal force', but what a bloody nonsense that is.

I finished the course with ninety-eight out of a hundred in law. This was very handy. I had memorised all the definitions. I'd learned it all off by heart. I thought to do the job, you need to get the knowledge, and then you'll be able to tell others. Anyway, off I went.

On my first day, after getting the bus, I was presented with my uniform. It almost felt like fancy dress, and I was very conscious of it. Even more so when I rode to C Division on my bicycle. I was sometimes late. In those days, on a bike, people would stop you in the street. I'd try and explain that I couldn't stop, as I wasn't in my division, and try to cycle off quickly. So, I decided it would be best to get a car. I could be invisible then. Eventually, I did. I became a divisional driver.

In my first year, I was taught all the basic stuff, working alongside long-standing officers. These had been there since the war years. They were military people and they didn't like the fact that I was a bit sloppy when saluting. I got passed by all of them eventually, because I was good at the job. Probation lasted for two years and the senior staff loved to remind you of this. They seemed to get a kick out of keeping you down, making sure you stay in your place. You couldn't make any mistakes. I soon got used to walking the beat. We had to keep our wits about us, and always look out for the oddity. The nights were the best, because at night time it's quiet. I won't go through all the commendations I got, but I do remember thinking, *I'll make this job work.*

One day, with Ruth still being in Cardiff, I decided to head back home to see her. I booked a long weekend off. It was Friday, Saturday and Sunday, and back on Monday.

She was now living in a flat in Partridge Road. I hitchhiked from Coventry. By the time I got to her front door, I just collapsed, I was so tired.

'What the hell are you doing?' she asked.

'I've come to see you,' I replied.

'Why didn't you get the bus?'

'I don't have any money.'

'And why have you brought the dog,' Ruth asked, pointing at the mutt sitting beside me.

'We both hitchhiked together.'

Anyway, I was there for a couple of days. We just went to the pub, had a couple of drinks and I walked the dog. One day I came back to Partridge Road carrying some food and there was a chap outside. He was breaking into a car, right in front of me.

'Excuse me, you shouldn't be doing that,' I said.

Of course, all the language started, with the f-offs. I told him I was a police officer, although I had no jurisdiction at all. While there, I was just an ordinary person. But I apprehended him. The police station was down the road in Clifton Street. I took him down there and went in, and this sergeant looked at me, with almost a glum disposition.

'What are you doing?' he asked. 'Why didn't you just leave him alone? You've got to get back to Coventry. What are you doing down here?'

But they arrested him and he was charged and went to court. About two months later, I realised that I would have to return to give evidence. But he pleaded guilty, thank goodness and I didn't have to come down.

After my stay with Ruth, I had to make my way back to Coventry, hitchhiking again. This time it was disastrous. Time was getting short. My shift was going to start at 10pm, so I had all day to get back up there. Then, somewhere in the middle of nowhere, a car pulled up, with two lovely girls in it. They took pity on me. I was all covered up. They were young, my age and asked if they could help. They said they were going to Coventry. I explained I was a police officer and had to be back by 10pm. They weren't worried and said we had plenty of time. Well, having plenty of time, we stopped at a pub. They were lovely girls and if I'd been single I would have taken them both home! I told them I was engaged, but that didn't put them off. They asked for my name and address. I said no, that I was PC402 and I had to get back by 10pm or I'd be hung. Well, we just had a drink and parted ways. I don't know if they'd remember me.

Well, I got back literally half an hour before my shift started. I still had the dog with me, so I put him in the common room, with all the police boxes. Just like the TARDIS in *Doctor Who*. I put the dog in a police box and told him to stay there, hoping he wouldn't move. You would get inspectors visit from time to time and I knew if anyone came along I'd get reprimanded. Despite being in a police box he wasn't a police dog. I didn't really do a proper job that night, as I had to keep taking the dog out to do his business. I decided to never again hike down to Cardiff. I got a van in the end, paid for the petrol and went down. I did a year of that. Ruth and I got married a year later in 1963.

I wasn't a military type, like all the officers. Some of them had serious problems. One used to get panic attacks at any accident. His name was Inspector Philip Orange, or Pip Orange, we called him. He was a lovely guy, good-natured, but he had come out of the army with serious PTSD. You'd be in the car with him, maybe on the bypass and the alarm would go off because there'd been an accident and he'd say, 'Officer, drop me off now, at the next corner.'

But we had one case, where he couldn't get out of it. As we arrived at the scene of an accident, it was obvious that a tanker had overturned. There was lots of oil, two cars involved and dead bodies. Of course, your training kicks in, but he jumped out of the car and said he was immediately going back to his office. He took the car and left me there by myself.

I rang control. It was Pete James on the switchboard.

He said, 'Is it Pip?'

I explained he was on his way back to the office, but told Pete not to worry and we covered for him. They got another car out to help me and, thank God, a policeman on patrol was coming around the corner, so I had some help. It took about two hours to sort that out. By the time you finish your shift, you're tired and you haven't eaten and you've got to get back home. Ruth often wasn't happy, waiting for me. She told me that later.

I was a good police officer and I was always busy looking for criminals. We typically had twelve officers on any one shift. Seven were maybe normal, doing the job, the rest were just putting in the time. There was one officer, PC1 was his number. All he used to do was go around the hotels and get lost. I didn't want to be with him.

Like many police officers, I saw the criminal as my enemy. I often thought, *I'll catch the bastard*, and I did. I'd arrest people at night, shining my flashlight into the darkness. The first crime I dealt with alone was in the middle of Coventry, about half past twelve at night. I forget the name of the street, but there was a working men's club. I was bored to death. I shone my torch on this Mini, which was parked in this club's car park. There was nothing suspicious, but suddenly I noticed the number plate and that the tax wasn't right. It's just something you check. I went back to the station and filed a report and finished my shift at 6am. After I'd finished and gone home in the morning, a guy on the next shift, called George Arnott, from CID, arrested a person when they came back to that car. They'd found out that this red Mini, with false plates on, was a stolen vehicle. So the driver got arrested.

Well, by the time I got back on shift the next night, all sorts was going off; phones ringing all the time, and I asked what was happening. Between my shifts, they'd arrested nine more people, including some in Germany, Luxembourg and France, after discovering a whole criminal ring, stealing cars and moving these cars around Europe… a whole lot of them. CID took over, but I got a commendation. It was just one small incident I was involved with, but it mushroomed. I've known police officers who have stopped cars, discovered the car is stolen, but let them drive off. Some of them are just young cadets with no experience of the world. I'd had some experience, going to sea and doing various jobs around Cardiff and Penarth, but I hadn't really wanted to join the police, despite all my efforts to do so. I did it because Ruth's mother wanted me to have a better job than being a deck-hand on a ship!

Ruth had previously been courting a boy who was in the Royal Navy. His name was Tony Coulthard. He was an engineer and a Catholic. I thought I had no chance. But Ruth's mother liked me, and she thought Coulthard was a bit boring. But she wanted something better for her daughter. And when Ruth and I did get together, Mrs Chapman, her mother, asked me to wait a couple of years before getting engaged. She was keen for me to find a better job and it was she who recommended the police force. I got a nasty letter from Coulthard once and I sometimes wind Ruth up about it. She'll ask me what it said. It was something like, 'If he's messing with my girl, I'll see him one night on a dark street.'

But, one time, Ruth came into the kitchen and told her mother, 'Mam, that's the boy I'm going to marry.'

My head went through the roof. Nobody had ever said anything so good before. Mrs Chapman knew she'd lost the fight then, but as the years went by she mellowed and she did tell me in conversation, privately, once, 'Robert, you're the best of the bunch.'

I replied that all the rest had either got divorced or run away! She saw the humour in me and she was okay about it. She'd had it tough. Her husband had been gassed and shot in World War I and used to sit in the kitchen, gasping for breath. I think Mrs Chapman believed that there would be longevity in my marriage to Ruth.

But, let's get back to my police days. There used to be a police box opposite the Co-Op. Well, I heard this noise, so I rang Pete James on the switchboard.

'Pete, someone is breaking into the Co-Op,' I said.

He said he'd send a car, but I told him not to send one too quickly. He was concerned there were spiked railings for me to get over, but I told him not to worry about that and jumped over the Co-Op railings. I went around a corner and two blokes were having a go at the door, trying to rip it off. Okay, I had two to deal with now. I shone the torch on my helmet and called out. Well, they jumped. I shouted out to my imaginary friend.

'John, keep that dog back for goodness sake. He'll tear them apart.'

And the two of them came quietly. I cuffed them both together. Then I walked around the corner at the end and there was nobody there you see. But, by that time Pete had called the car and as I got around there the car was pulling outside the gates.

I was told off by the chief inspector for going onto the premises. I explained that I didn't want them to get away. Well, of course that caused another row.

But as things went on and on and on, I was picking up points, you see. Then I got offered a car, which I thought was a good idea at the time and would save walking around. I failed the test the first time. You've got to drive through Coventry and they didn't mess about. It was a Humber Hawk, with the gear underneath the steering wheel, and the handbrake on the other side! Why they put the handbrake there, I don't know.

When you got to traffic lights, it's in gear. I took the handbrake off and 'whack', the stick came down across me. So, I'd failed, because I had no hands on the steering wheel. We were bloody stationary. I passed the second time okay. The Humber Hawk was a heavy old car, but I thought it was great. I was off now.

At my first accident I didn't know what to do. I turned up and my first thought was, *Please send for a policeman.* I said to this man, 'Go back up the road, there's a phone box. Ring them and ask for an ambulance and when you've done it, come back, so we can sort the accident out.'

As it went on and on, I got more confident and more relaxed, but the first one was terrible. You've got to get people in their right places. One sitting there... I'd say, 'I'll come back to you.' Another one there, who needs an ambulance. You've got to work it all that in your head. But, it does come.

And sometimes it could be funny…

Every Saturday night you had to deal with fights. They broke out everywhere in the streets. It was hard to control it, because everyone would be running about. *Carry on, knock yourselves out,* I used to sometimes think. And they would often do just that. I had to go to the hospital with a suspect once. I was handcuffed to him while he had his nose stitched back on. He'd been in a fight and probably been glassed.

'He seems quiet,' I said.

'Yes, but wait 'til the bloody anaesthetic wears off!'

Another time, at an accident, there was a chap sitting there and he only had one leg. I asked if he was all right and he said he was and that he'd already asked my colleague to go and get his other leg, out of the car. I thought he'd actually lost his leg for real, but he was quite nonchalant about it, saying, 'Just go and get my leg please officer, and I'll be all right then.'

Of course, it was a wooden leg, and they wound me up about this back at the station. That's the black humour, you see. Admittedly, there was a lot of death and destruction. Something happened every day in Coventry. We were very, very busy. Eventually, of course, other officers started asking me what to do.

I had the van one day – a Black Maria. I had nobody with me and I'd left it for a bit. I got in trouble for that, because I'd gone to help a woman being raped on the stairs.

What would you do? Well, I was told to come back, put the van in, take the bike out, and work a twelve-beat. It was my punishment. The sergeant put me on a beat way up in Warwickshire on Oldsey Old Road, Fletchamstead Highway, going towards Birmingham. It was miles out. I actually didn't mind that. It was quiet.

But at half past one in the morning, I got a call to go in. I said I was due to be on an early breakfast shift and this wound the sergeant up a bit. Eventually he let me go and I took the car and off I went. I never got out of the car then. They couldn't get rid of me.

But I also enjoyed driving the van. Once, I'd had someone with me, but they'd buggered off. There was a report of a stolen vehicle in Birmingham. I found the car first; it had been abandoned on a side road to the main road. It smelled of beer. Once again, I was by myself. I saw four other blokes walking back from a petrol station.

Well, I didn't know what they were doing or where they were going. I couldn't be sure that they were the thieves, but that was my assumption. They had beer cans and were all drunk. Perhaps because they'd run out of petrol. They were also carrying fuel. It just didn't look normal. They were on the road thumbing a lift. So I thought, *I can't ignore them, can I?* So, I pulled up and took my hat off. They didn't react as though I was a copper. Maybe they thought I was a bus conductor. So I asked, 'Where are you going, lads?' They were going my way so I told them that they could get in the back. Well, of course, once you shut that back door, there's no way to open it from the inside. I turned the van around and off I went. They realised we were going the wrong way. I told them to calm down, saying I was taking a short cut. I got the phone going then and rang into Pete. He was always on the switchboard.

'Pete, Pete,' I said. 'I've got some angry Irishmen here.'

Well, they seemed to wake up then and realise they were in a police van. By the time I got to the station, they were really rocking that van. You could turn those vans over really quite easily, if you wanted to. I was on two wheels at one point. I got into the yard, stopped and jumped out quickly. There were dents in the van. Anyway, five coppers came out and I said, 'Get on with it!' They opened the back door and the Irishmen piled out. They were understandably upset. I was inside, getting a cup of tea. They started fighting, but the others got them in the cells and gave them a cup of tea. The language on the tapes was unbelievable, but they were all laughing in the end.

It went to court about a month or two later. It was judge and jury – twelve of them. Well, that time, I was driven to the court by Inspector Deeming. We were sort of friends by then. He was all right. Another military man. You had to salute him. Anyway, he took me to court and he said to me, being quite posh now, 'Now look, Robert, when you go in there, remember your training. He'll come at you like a bloody Rottweiler, this barrister.'

I was shaking. I mean I was on the stand now, giving evidence. You have to state your name and rank, 402 and I was in uniform. But I was still the same bloke, Bob Maddocks from Penarth.

The four men were in the dock. They're over one side, the jury's over the other side and the barristers are up front. I got up to give evidence and I thought, *This is not going to go well. They're not going to believe what happened.* The barrister was fed up with me. He flourished his hands at the jury and said, 'Are we expected to believe that you, 402, arrested these Irishmen on a wet, windy night on a bypass and took them back to the station?'

Well, one bloke in the dock jumped up and said, 'He fuckin' well did, the bastard!' And they were all laughing.

Well, the barrister turned against me and tried again, 'How are we expected to believe that you arrested all these men by yourself?'

I replied that I only had one pair of handcuffs, making

a joke if it. There was a lot of laughter by then and he decided he had no more questions. They were criminals, but they knew they'd met their match. They were angry, but they went down for a year. They'd done more than one crime, and once one is discovered, others get added on you see. I'd left before they were found guilty, but I'd been shaking like a leaf. It was my first time with a jury looking at you. Magistrates Court is easy, but when you get a jury looking at you, you're nervous.

Eventually I went to every court in the land, even the coroners court. The years flew by. I got a call once to get to a scene quick. Someone had committed suicide on a second floor. I remember the house. It was a woman. She had put her head in a gas oven and she'd definitely died. They go blue. She'd left a note, saying, 'Joe is downstairs in the coal bunker.' I was reading this, thinking, *Joe is downstairs in the coal bunker?*

'Christ, get down there, in case there's another one.'

My mate shot down the stairs, then he says, 'It's a budgie.'

To save the budgie's life, she'd taken Joey, the budgie, down to the coal bunker. Well, that came out in court. Well, of course, when you give evidence in court, you've got the relatives there. They said they wanted to thank 'the young officer' for his conduct. But, I was just doing my job. You do the job: it's always someone else's mother or father, or somebody.

I saw a young chap die by accident on the bypass. He smashed into the back of a lorry on his push bike. I was actually standing on the corner when it happened. It was my third accident and I didn't know what to do. As the lorry turned the back axle went 'BANG!'. I could see it all happening – the bike went into the lorry and the boy went head first into the side and was stuck there. I ran across the road and the lorry driver jumped out. I calmed him down, told him I'd seen what had happened and put him back in his cab. I ran across the road to the phone box. The ambulance turned up and then it all got going. The ambulance men were all young, like me. I told them the casualty was in the back of the lorry with his head buried in it. They told me not to touch him and that he was dead. He was still held on the bike by the rat-traps: the clips that go over your feet on the pedals. As a result, he was held up, still in the cycling position, but dead. Turned out it was his twenty-first birthday.

He lived in a place on Kenilworth Road, just off the bypass. It was my responsibility to tell the parents. It wasn't the only time I had to do that sort of thing. Later in life, I was the personnel officer at the Wheal Jane mine. I had to go and tell a woman that her husband had been cut in half. I guess, because I seemed knowledgeable, this was always dumped on me. Maybe I was. Everyone's always said to me, 'Robert, you've got more sense than so and so…'

Was I more mature? I don't know. It does help you grow up, being away at sea; away from the comfort of home.

Chapter Seven
Married Life Begins

Ruth and I got married in 1963 when I was working in Coventry. My best man was Roger Brown, a colleague in Coventry City Police. He did it willingly. He came down from Coventry and stayed in a hotel, somewhere in St Agnes. We married in Cornwall, because that's where Ruth's parents were then living. The church was called Our Lady Star of the Sea, a Catholic church. There were only a few people there. My mother wasn't there, because she'd died sometime before, and my sister didn't turn up, because my father told her not to, though I didn't know this at the time. She had to do what she was told. And he didn't turn up, of course: horrible.

Ruth's sister, Barbara Chapman, wasn't there, because she was in Canada at the time. That was a good thing really. I didn't like her much. Barbara was twelve when Ruth was born and it was obvious that she was jealous of her. Anyway, we all went to the church in my car, a Zephyr Zodiac. Mrs Chapman, Ruth's mum, was very happy, because she'd got to know me and trusted me then.

Another woman did turn up and I asked her who she was. She replied that she just went to all the weddings at that church. I think she might have been the priest's sister. Also there was Nick, Ruth's friend from Cardiff. He came down, just to be there.

The wedding was simple. We had no money, so Ruth had made her own wedding dress. The priest was Father O'Reagan. I remember he talked with me, trying to get me to relax. I was stressed and so was Ruth. Father O'Reagan talked to me about his car. He said he had a problem with it and had to get new tyres the next day, so he wouldn't get told off by the police. It was an odd subject considering where we were, but he was just trying to relax me. Anyway, we got through it and signed the bits of paper. I've got a picture of us on the wedding day. Me in my suit that cost thirty bob. We all look very lovely.

There weren't many people at the reception either, but Roger Brown was there of course. It was in the St Agnes Hotel. He gave a speech. Mrs Chapman was a little unsure. The marriages of her two older daughters had ended in divorce, and she possibly felt she was losing another daughter.

The honeymoon night was normal. I think we went into St Ives for the evening. I went into a pub and had half a lager. Ruth wasn't very happy about that.

'I don't know what I've done. I've lost my freedom,' she said.

I think she meant it. You never really know with Ruth. She was young and stressed. I think she was just realising she wasn't free anymore and I told her we were in it together now. It's all very well, the romance of getting married, but when you're married, you're married, aren't you? It's maybe not for life, although it has been for us. I don't know how to explain it. We decided to try it out and I did my best. My mother had brought me up correctly.

We did have a short honeymoon. Well, it was more of a day out because I had to get back to work. Arriving in Perranporth, I parked the car in the street, near the coast. We found a Bed & Breakfast, just for two nights. I still had the dog with me. He had to stay in the car. But he was very good. He did as he was told.

After the wedding, we got a little flat up in Coventry. It was in a horrible place. In Bell Green, in the middle of nowhere. It was a fourth-storey flat. Ruth hated it there. They put police officers there to keep the rabble down I think. There was a lot of smog in Coventry in those days too. You couldn't see to get in the police car sometimes.

But there we were, two young people, starting married life together. I had a job to do and I was making a success of it.

Time went on and our first child, Rachel, was born, on 23rd May 1964.

What a traumatic event that was. It was raining and foggy, plus the smog from all the coal fires. I got home early morning, off a night shift, and we called for the midwife. She turned up late. My wife's sister, Barbara, had also turned up to help because she was a midwife herself. She was actually sick in the room while the baby was being born. She was single and never got married. But she was sick. Then she went back home to Cornwall. When our midwife turned up, she couldn't get the gas and air machine to work.

But Ruth got on with it by herself and a little girl appeared. I thought it was wonderful – one of life's great experiences. Yes, the flat was horrible, but life went on. We moved into town, to a better place, near the bypass. I didn't know at the time though, that Ruth was really very unhappy. She was at home all day with the baby and I didn't realise that brought a lot of stress.

My daughter was, not difficult exactly, but it felt like she wasn't our own daughter. It was hard to talk about it, but Ruth said to me one day that, if it wasn't for the fact that the baby had been born in the flat, she wouldn't believe she had the right baby. She just seemed completely detached. There was no love or comfort to be found there. Ruth tried to cope, but having your first child can be difficult and I was on night shifts all the time. It didn't help, of course, that

Ruth's parents were miles away in Cornwall and we were all by ourselves.

She went to grammar school later and university after that. She turned out to be the black sheep of the family. It's true. She was a horrible child – annoying, screaming and shouting and belligerent. She didn't like us. Ruth used to say to me that she didn't know what to do and we had no guidance from anybody. My daughter grew up of course, but I haven't seen her for fifteen years now.

Chapter Eight
More Police Work

Anyway, I digress. There are millions of stories from being in the police. I can't recount them all. There were so many incidents and every day something was different. I became immune to road accidents. Other times it was almost comedic, but you become hardened to it.

About halfway through my time, I passed my advanced driving test to be a divisional car driver. This kept me busy.

Crime is everywhere. I remember a drunk woman. She parked on the zig-zags and was wearing her pyjamas. The copper stopped her and she started biting his arm. In the pub, I was watching it from the front window.

I was a shy person, but as a police officer, I did see many interesting things. In those times, the police cars were run into the ground. The engines never stopped. You'd finish work, the next shift would come along, and they'd ask if there was any damage. You'd say no, and off they would go again. The engines never stopped.. I suppose that's how it had to be. It was a working police car. One time, I was driving an inspector and chief inspector back from somewhere. They used the cars as a bloody taxi service sometimes.

Well, I was heading back to the police station and I stopped at the lights. I didn't want to make any mistakes with the inspectors behind me, but the stick came off in my hand. I was just a young kid. Unbelievable! So, now I'm in first gear – that's all I've got. The lights changed and they looked at me. I couldn't move, but eventually, I got onto a slight slope.

'Officer, is there a problem?' I hear from the back.

'Well, yes, sir,' I said and I gave him the stick.

They were embarrassed, sitting in a police car doing fifteen mph on a forty-mile-an-hour stretch of road. The police station felt like it was a million miles away. I called Pete and explained what had happened and that I would be a little late. I could hear them all laughing their heads off at the police station. The inspector suggested waving the traffic past, but I replied that no one would overtake us. No one would overtake a police car! It was a busy road and, at that speed, there must have been a hundred and fifty cars behind us at one point, but I lost track. I got into the right-hand lane to use a roundabout.

Over the radio I could hear the staff all going, 'vroooooom, vroooom, vroooom' and laughing at me.

As I arrived at the yard, the two in the back jumped out. They were bloody livid.

'Right, officer,' one of them said, 'get this car down to A Division and get a new car.'

Well, that was nice. I explained that I couldn't drive the car any further, but he insisted that I get the car replaced. So, I had to ride a push bike down there. I ended up with a brand-new car. It was spotless and I didn't want to drive the thing! There was so much laughter on that day. It just seemed that things were always happening to me.

One morning, Inspector Deeming turns up and tells me he's putting a new officer with me, PC Drew. He'd come directly from university. Now, fair enough, this was a compliment, putting this young graduate with me, but PC Drew told me right off that he was there to learn from me, but that he'd be an inspector by the next month. Well, I showed him what

I did and, you know what, I had him for the whole month! He asked me how I seemed to know everything that was going on, to which I replied, 'Well, we're on the same street every day, aren't we?'

And, you know what, he did become an inspector, Inspector bloody Drew, and it was less than three months. They moved him up the ranks, despite not having any knowledge of police work, other than what he'd read in the manual. I was later told by Superintendent Murray that they'd put him with me because I was felt to be the officer who would teach him how to do the job properly. That was nice, wasn't it? I was just doing the job.

Let me tell you about the ambassador. It was about halfway through my time with Coventry City Police. One day, I was on the bypass in Coventry. It goes from Coventry to Birmingham. Now, coming from Birmingham – although we didn't know this – there was an ambassador on his way to London. I didn't know any of this. I was just on patrol in a car. I was supposed to pick up the reserve officers, but they didn't want to come with me because they thought it would mean too much work. So this time, I'm driving in the Humber and I saw this other vehicle, pulled over on the side of the road. I saw the diplomatic plates on it and thought it looked interesting. I pulled up behind it and walked up to the car. It was a fabulous car, with the driver on the other side, and in the back was a man holding a suitcase with a chain around it. I took all this in quickly and asked if they needed help.

'Oh, officer, thank God,' the driver said.

He explained the man in the back was the American ambassador and they had broken down. They had been trying to contact the police and thought the service was very fast, but it was pure luck that I just happened to be there. I asked what the problem was and the driver told me that they had to get to London airport by a certain time. I was on a six 'til two shift, I remember that. I quickly rang it into Divisional Headquarters. Pete was on the counter. He said he'd been trying to get hold of me to explain about this vehicle going through our division and that we were to let it through quickly. He described the vehicle and I explained I was standing beside it and that it had broken down.

Pete started ringing around and the chief inspector and chief constable got involved. I soon received instructions from the chief constable that I was to take over. He instructed me to leave their car there and it would be picked up by someone else. I was then to take the driver and ambassador to the border with the next county, where we would lose jurisdiction. This was only about two to three miles away. I queried this and was told again to just get him to the border, where there would be another car from another division to take him to London.

So, off I went. The ambassador was a lovely guy. He smelled of perfume, which I thought showed he'd got some standards. The driver was very nervous but thanked me. We were driving along and chatting. He explained that if they didn't make their plane they were stuffed. He said it was a matter of national importance. I asked what he meant. He had important documents locked in the suitcase, you see. Anyway, I got him to the border. At a roundabout, another car was waiting, with blue lights flashing. We quickly exchanged pleasantries. He thanked me and was gone.

I carried on with my normal job, dealing with prisoners and looking for criminals. I finished at two o'clock. I arrived home and Ruth was in the kitchen making me a cup of tea.

'You've been busy today,' she said.

'Pardon?' I said.

'It was on the news. There was an incident in Coventry and you were mentioned.'

Before the ambassador got on the plane he'd given a press conference and praised the assistance he received from the Coventry City Police, especially Officer 402. The chief constable got the official thank you, even though I'd done the driving, but that's life.

I was well in with the chief constable then. I was popular, but not everyone liked that. One time, I attended the Lord Mayor's dinner and they were all messing with me and asking me if I'd enjoyed it. I said I didn't want to attend and would rather be out working, just to wind them up.

Ruth said, 'You do get about.' That's true, you do in a police car. I've dealt with deaths, murders, mayhem. You approach any incident and you've got to be prepared for anything. We didn't have mobile phones then. I had a car radio, YN24, Fancy me remembering those numbers.

I couldn't really live on £15 a week. I went to see Superintendent Murray at the police station, two floors up. I offered my resignation and he called me up there. They call you by your number, even though you've got a name. Superintendent Murray said he wouldn't accept my resignation, but I replied that I had to go.

'You can't go, 402,' he said. 'It will get better. We don't want to let you go. There's a place for you here in Coventry, because you are an outstanding officer.'

I said, 'Sir, £15 a week isn't enough. It was difficult getting in and now I can't get out.' I was making a joke again.

'Look, Robert, 402, where are you going to go?'

I explained my wife was very stressed and that Ruth's parents lived in Cornwall. I suggested that I was going to maybe join the police down there. I tried to, but they turned me down. An inspector in Oakhampton told me that I only wanted to go there for a cushy life. I pointed out that he too was sitting down there with a cushy life. Well, he didn't like that.

Anyway, I found out that Coventry wouldn't let me go. You see, it's not easy. I discovered later on that if you're rubbish, they will get rid of you. But I was good. I had commendations. I went to the Lord Mayor's dinner. It's luck in a way. You fall into things or upon things and it happens just right.

They accepted my resignation in the end. Coventry was never really my home. It was in the Midlands, there was no sea around me, and when you've got the coast around you, you know where you are. Ruth wanted to be with her parents, who lived in Cornwall, with Barbara in a lovely place called Rosewall. I had about £200 of savings, so off we went to Cornwall.

Chapter Nine
Cornwall Part I

After I quit the police force, we went to Cornwall. Ruth was pregnant again and Julian was born on 21st October 1966, the same date as the Aberfan disaster.

We'd stayed for a while with Mr and Mrs Chapman, waiting for something to come up. I grabbed the first job I could. There was a company called The Wesleyan & General Insurance Company. They were advertising for agents to go and sell insurance. They were at 57, Lemon Street, in Truro. It was a big office and George Lake was the manager. I went in and I got the job straight away.

They guide you through the process by giving you a round, showing you the location, and then you take it from there. They supplied a car and I sold door-to-door throughout Cornwall. Most of my work was done in the evenings and the wages were appalling, but you made it up on commission. I was on £100 a week at one point, flogging policies like hell.

I had one hundred homes at one point, from which I had to regularly collect the payments. You'd go into one house where they might be watching *Coronation Street*, see the first bit of that, go to the next house and catch the next bit, and by the end of the evening, I'd see the entire programme. Some of them would come to the door, but others would just shout, 'Hello!' because they were glued to the TV set.

I met all sorts of people and there was a lot of poverty.

The customers were in housing estates. At one house I went to in Falmouth, they opened the door and the stair bannister had gone. Apparently, they had burned it to keep warm. I remember one house I visited and the whole family was stark naked in the kitchen having a meal. They seemed to think it was normal. It's not normal, is it? I thought okay and I still asked for the premium. I said, 'See you next week,' and walked out. The Cornish could be very strange people. I told Ruth that story, but she didn't believe it.

If you had a cheque to give someone because a policy had paid out, you'd take it down to them. They'd be very happy and that was a good time to drum up more business. I didn't push it, but I was a chatterbox, and I used to just talk to people. Some were polite, some were rude, and some didn't want to know us.

I also sold some policies and provided the cover notes for a dodgy car insurance company run by a guy called Suvindra. Not everyone could afford Wesleyan prices and Wesleyan didn't want to take on those who might not pay, but Suvindra did. I did that for about a year. It wasn't a great job. I didn't like it much, but it paid okay and enabled me to buy my first house.

We had to leave Mrs Chapman's house because we were imposing on her. A tiny one-bedroom cottage came up for sale near her, called Woodlands. I bought it from a lady called Mrs Mitchell. They were asking £1000 for it. Looking back now, even if it sounds ridiculous, £1000 was a lot of money then. I went to Wesleyan & General and they said they'd give me a mortgage, which I got. The mortgage was £4 a month. It was a one-and-a-half-bedroom place on the side of the road, about half a mile from Ruth's mum at Mount Hawk. That was nice for Ruth and it was a start.

My son Julian was born there. This time, the midwife came on time. She was a lot more organised than the first one. She said to me, 'You've done your work, now bugger off, go on…'

That was the usual thing, so I did as I was told.

He was a brilliant little boy and very different to my daughter. They had different personalities, like chalk and cheese. As they were growing up, my daughter didn't seem to ever want to be involved in anything, but she was always bullying my son. He brushed it off and got through it all. When he was little he used to play with Lego and Meccano, often connecting the batteries and lights in a circuit. He was very bright. He was both practical and academic.

We never had any holidays when the children were young. None at all. We couldn't afford them and I was doing up houses all the time. Birthdays weren't very exciting either, but life went on. I wasn't doing brilliantly and we went through some rough times. I guess that's not surprising with my lifestyle. I do blame myself, but Ruth stuck by me. I say that because we used to go to a local pub in St Agnes and there was a boy there who was very keen on her. He was a carpenter, well-established, and he had a nice big house. Anyway, I drove past our house one day and there was a bike parked outside. I asked Ruth about it and she said she didn't know what I was talking about. The truth was that this man had attempted to seduce Ruth. She denied all this, but he wanted her to go and live with him and Ruth was thinking about it. I couldn't believe that. I was devastated that day and told Ruth she had to decide what she wanted. She didn't go. I think she more or less decided that day that it was better to stick with what she'd got. Well, that passed anyway. Mrs Chapman told her off, but it passed and we settled down then.

I decided that the Wesleyan & General thing wasn't for me – it was bloody boring. I had to move on again. This was around 1969. I replied to an advertisement in Truro for Consolidated Gold Fields, a South African company. They were re-opening a mine in Baldhu. It was quite a popular move and we'd heard about it.

They planned to first sink the shafts, a task assigned to

Thysens, a German firm. Their strategy involved descending into the depths and then reopening the old workings, as the mine was being revived. I collaborated with Thysens for about a month, but it was a brief stint. I lost hearing in one ear from the underground explosions. Looking back, it seems utterly reckless; I must have been out of my mind.

A chap called Mr Gamble took me on, although he did ask me if I was sure, saying that I wasn't really built for it. Well, I thought I was quite strong, but once I got started, I realised what he was talking about. It was a tin mine and there was rock and lots of water. The water ran out into the sea and there was a big flood risk. That's why they'd closed it down before.

Anyway, after Mr Gamble took me on I went down there, but I only lasted a month. I couldn't do any more. There was a German bloke in charge and I got on well with him. He told me to get on the shaft sinker and stand on it while it went up and down.

'As you do it, this quick-drying cement gets poured in behind you to line the shaft,' he said. 'You have to keep going all the way down. Right down to the bottom, right?'

I realised I was just too slender for the work. They were all huge, hard blokes and I wasn't hard. After two rounds with Thysens, I couldn't do it! Well, they laughed at me going up and down, hanging on. You have to adjust it too, to make it go down again. And you do that for four hours…

Then they ram the dynamite down the hole. It's all fired by an electrical connection, with the middle going first, then the second one and the idea is that it clears the space, without blowing the walls out. It was horrific work and it was dangerous.

I remember once I was preparing it all and the water started coming in. I said, 'What the hell is that? Why is the water coming in?'

But actually, it helped to clear things out. You need to get out of the way, of course. Typically, you jump in this big bucket called a Witches' Cauldron, which hoists you up. As you're rising, the water comes in and it gets under the bucket. Once you reach the top you dash around the corner to a shed, blow the dynamite, which you can hardly hear. Of course, after that, there are balls of rock to clear out.

The money was good and I met some great people, but I was done with it all. My back hurt and I'd gone deaf in one ear. I still am. I couldn't do it anymore.

After finishing my last day, I drove home in deathly silence. I couldn't hear a thing, not even the engine rattling away, and I had a rusty old van then. I got home and went to bed. I slept for two days – my back was killing me.

After that, I went to work on the coast at Nancekuke, near Portreath. They made all the poisonous gas for the war. It was a chemical place, a subsidiary of Portland Down in Wiltshire. It was highly secretive and I had to sign the Official Secrets Act. I was a security officer, patrolling the place day and night, with six others, all ex-policemen. I did that for a while and it was boring as hell, but then I got a message from my mate at Thysens. He told me that the mine was now opening and they were looking for people. He said he'd thought of me, as I'd be better off running the mine than digging the holes!

Anyway, I got a job at the Wheal Jane mine. I was hired by Jeff Clamp, a nice bloke. He asked if I could provide security. I had six men in mind from Nancekuke. I asked them if they wanted to come across and they all agreed! Jeff was still there, but he wasn't in charge anymore and we had to discuss the employment of the new security team with his replacement, Mike Matthews. He was very awkward and argumentative, asking what sort of money we wanted. He didn't want to take me on, but Jeff convinced him. I managed to keep the job and brought all these people over with me.

I was a personnel officer... in the posh area! But, because I'd been underground, I knew the layout. I used to go down every day to see the progress too. It was amazing. They weren't after lithium then. It was tin. They just dumped the lithium. That makes me laugh, as it's so valuable now. They did find some specks of silver and gold as well, but not much.

I had a bit of responsibility, the money was good, and Ruth was pleased. The mining company had two ships: coasters that would take the tin up north somewhere. I was in charge of that and security, and the sixty-seven miners that I took on, who came down from the Midlands for work. They lived in sixty-seven houses on St Clements Street in Truro. It was a new estate that was built for them.

While I was doing that job, we moved from Woodlands to a place in Vicarage Road in St Agnes. We just wanted a bigger place to be honest. It was a three-bedroom house, with a rear entrance and parking. The guy who was living there at the time had been renting it and was moving on.

The owner was a dentist. I went to see him and sat in the dentist's chair while talking to him about buying his house… and getting my teeth done. I'm not making it up.

I can't remember his name. It might have been McMann. I managed to do a deal with him anyway. I got a mortgage and we moved in.

But Mike Matthews (he's dead now) didn't like me, because I was too popular. I was doing the job, but he said because I hadn't been trained as a personnel officer, he would put me on probation for two years. I told him to just carry on, but all the staff were saying, 'Watch yourself, Robert.'

At lunchtime, 12.30-1pm, we used to go down to Blackwater to a local pub. Some of the men would come down with me and I would sit with them, while some of the other office staff would sit in another room and look through the hatch at me. They asked why I didn't come and sit with them and I told them I was happy sitting with the working men. I was a working man. Well, Matthews didn't like that.

The next day he said to me, 'We've been looking at your van in the car park. It's disgusting. You need to change your vehicle because it's letting the side down.'

Oh, what a bastard he was. I had a Ford Escort mini-van. It was a rusty old van and it looked terrible, but it was mine and I didn't have any money. I said, 'If you give me the money for another one I will change it.' Of course, he didn't like that either. He was on at me all the time.

Now, Dave Littlejohn was a friend of mine, also an ex-police officer. He said, 'This bastard, you know, he doesn't know what he's doing. He's on your back, isn't he? Well, he's having an affair with one of the staff.'

'How do you know?' I asked.

'I caught him with her yesterday,' he replied. 'You've got something over him now, Bob.'

Now, I wasn't bothered, but Matthews told me he wouldn't promote me because I wasn't, as he put it, up to scratch with all the figures. I didn't say anything about the affair, but he knew that I knew and his attitude changed a bit after that.

He sacked another girl who wouldn't give in to his advances. She rang me one night and told me about this. She also told me the reason he didn't like me – that I was too popular. I asked what she was talking about, as I was just being me. She said he was jealous. Why was he like that? I don't know.

The next thing I knew, he asked me to pay out the miners last thing at night. They were on £500 each. I had over ten grand in the van once and I went out from St Agnes to the mine, at half past eleven at night and paid them out. All that money! They deserved it though. I was on £30 a week. I didn't have any money really, but it was interesting work.

In the end, the chief came out from South Africa to look

at the site. His name was Mr Tress and he was a nice guy. He'd heard about the things going on. He knew my background and that I had a good reputation there. He sacked Matthews and suggested, because everyone liked me, that I should be put in his place. I thought about it, but maybe too long. Anyway, somebody else got the job. He had a vacancy for a personnel officer in South Africa, but there they only had one officer per thousand miners, and a thousand people were applying, so I didn't do that. But I worked at Wheal Jane mine for about two years (up to 1973). Sadly, it's closed down now, but that's life.

Penarth Docks, 1930.

My grandfather in uniform. He was in the Home Guard.

HMS Glomous, June 8th 1940.

Uncle Harry was lost at sea, 1940.

Me, second on the left, next to Mr Parry, my history teacher.

Me and my grandfather on the River Ely, 1952.

My dad with drinking friends in Penarth pub. He's next to the bar.

My mam, 1950.

I spent time in the Panama Canal, 1956.

Mam with Ruth, 1958.

Me in Wood Street, Cardiff, 1958.

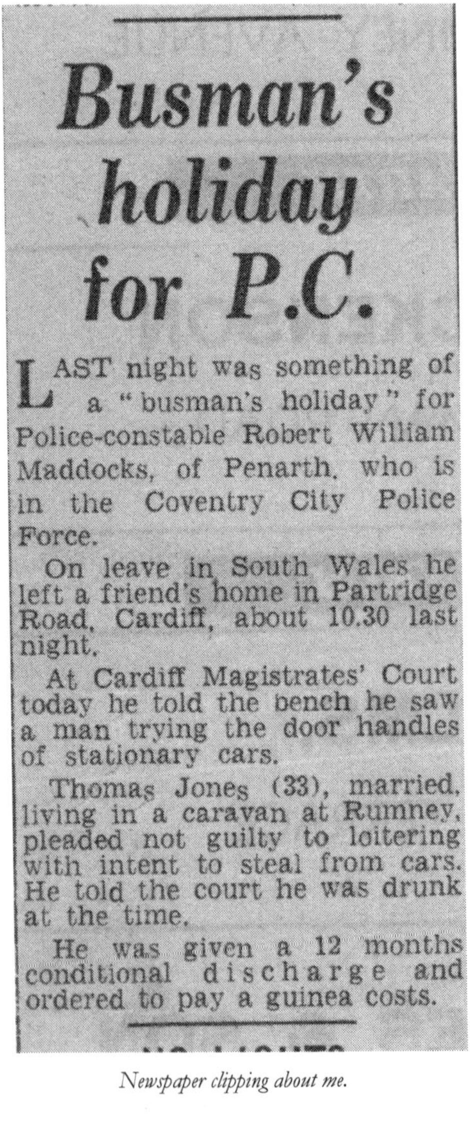

Busman's holiday for P.C.

LAST night was something of a "busman's holiday" for Police-constable Robert William Maddocks, of Penarth, who is in the Coventry City Police Force.

On leave in South Wales he left a friend's home in Partridge Road, Cardiff, about 10.30 last night.

At Cardiff Magistrates' Court today he told the bench he saw a man trying the door handles of stationary cars.

Thomas Jones (33), married, living in a caravan at Rumney, pleaded not guilty to loitering with intent to steal from cars. He told the court he was drunk at the time.

He was given a 12 months conditional discharge and ordered to pay a guinea costs.

Newspaper clipping about me.

LORD MAYOR'S PARLOUR
COUNCIL HOUSE
COVENTRY

TELEPHONE No. 25555

The Lord Mayor

(Alderman A. J. Waugh, J.P.)

has pleasure in inviting

P. C. R. MADDOCKS

to Dinner

in the Guildhall of St. Mary, Coventry,

on Tuesday, the 14th May, 1963,

at 7.15 for 7.45 p.m.

in appreciation of the work of the

City Police Force and the

Special Constabulary.

Dress: Informal

R.S.V.P.
(by enclosed card)

Aperitifs at
7.15 p.m.
Assembly Rooms.

Invitation to Lord Mayor's Dinner, 1963.

Me with Storm, Roath Park, 1962.

Ruth and myself getting married in Cornwall. Best man, PC Roger Brown, 1963.

On the way back to the UK from Australia, 1976.

YEFB National Final, Julian Maddocks, 1981.

Holly, with me and Hilary.

The Gatehouse, 2008.

Chapter Ten
Australia Bound

A few years before, we'd had a big bust-up with Ruth's sister, Barbara.

When we first went to Cornwall we stayed at my in-laws, until I found a house. Anyway, they had four daughters and Ruth was the youngest. The older two had both previously married but then divorced. Barbara, the third daughter, was twelve years older than Ruth, and she lived there as well. She was a nurse and a spinster. I couldn't get on with her at all.

Ruth's parents signed the house over to Barbara for tax purposes. We stayed there for about two months and I was very self-conscious about it, but Mrs Chapman was fine herself. One day, Barbara came home after work and was very argumentative.

Then she said to me, 'Robert, I want you to leave.'

I said, 'Pardon?' and Mrs Chapman asked Barbara what she'd said. Now, Mrs Chapman, who'd had all these daughters, loved me to bits and I liked her. She'd seen other husbands all walk away, but I was loyal as hell, even though Ruth could be difficult… still is.

Anyway, Mrs Chapman said, 'What did you say, Barbara?'

Mr Chapman was sat by the fire, coughing his heart out and I felt sorry for him. Barbara said he should apologise to me, but I felt honoured to know the guy. For Christ's sake, he'd been shot at in the war. It was obvious that she was jealous.

'It's my house you know,' Barbara said.

'Barbara, I'm aware of that, but is there a problem?'

Mrs Chapman told her to apologise, but she wouldn't. She was adamant about this. She just wanted me to leave. I agreed. No, I actually made an offer to go further than that. 'I'll leave the bloody country,' I suggested. And I meant it. I just had one stipulation.

'I give you my word. If you put the house back in your parent's name tomorrow, I'll drive you into Truro, to a solicitor, and I promise you I'll be gone by the next day. You will be rid of me.'

Anyway, she agreed to this. And the deed was done.

We eventually moved into 2 Vicarage Rd in St Agnes, still close to Ruth's parents. Sadly neither Ruth's parents nor Barbara ever came to visit us there.

While this wasn't the sole cause of our later move to Australia, the argument with Barbara had precipitated the idea, and although it meant Mrs Chapman lost another daughter, we still took the plunge.

Ruth's parents sold the house while we were gone. They were getting old. They bought another house, but Barbara never left. She was always there. She never got married. I can't really explain what she was like, but she was always around. Poor Mrs Chapman asked if I'd look after Barbara when they passed away and I said I would. Barbara had a stroke later on, not as bad as my wife's, but it affected her side. I went to see her and she said she wanted to come and live near me and Ruth. We were in Carmarthen at the time. I thought that could be dangerous, but I helped her sell the house – for a lot of money, £250,000, and helped her pack everything up. She came and stayed with us for a while, but that didn't last long. She wanted Ruth to cook for her and was generally an awful person.

I told her she'd have to find a house for herself, but

everywhere she went, she didn't like it. Ruth ended up giving her an ultimatum: Just buy something, no matter what it was like. Well, it was a horrible house, but Barbara didn't care. She said she was taking it, just to satisfy Ruth. She bought it with cash and offered them more money than they were asking for it. And it wasn't all her money to spend.

'Your mother will be turning in her grave,' I said.

Barbara recovered from her stroke quite well. She was a nasty piece of work, though. I still can't understand where it came from. I rang her one day to ask about something and she told me, 'I'm too busy at the moment.'

Ruth said I wasn't to ring her again and I've never heard from her since. She could be dead for all I know.

Ruth had been a teacher in Coventry before we had children. Australia desperately needed teachers, so it felt like the right time to go. I happily agreed. I'm a restless spirit. I was easily persuaded. If truth be told, I couldn't see myself progressing in this country.

The mining people were good to me. We had to sell the house. It was bought by a guy called Featherstone Harvey, a very posh man. He was an optician and he had plenty of money. He'd previously made an offer on a house further down the road, but had been turned down. We made a little profit from the sale, giving us some cash in the bank to get to Australia.

We have been back to Mt Hawk since, because Ruth's parents are buried there. We used to stay at a hotel on the corner, The Railway Inn. I actually played football for the pub team, the Railway Sleepers.

When I sold the house, even though the date of our departure was coming up, we had nowhere to go. That was when the Mining Company stepped in with temporary accommodation. The boss from South Africa arranged it: it was all free.

Beginning the process of getting to Australia, we wrote a letter to Australia House in London, telling them we wanted to emigrate. We had to go up there to London, for the interviews and such. I sat in a side street in the car with the kids when Ruth discussed getting a job. When she came back she announced said she was going to be Head of Department at a school in a place called Townsville, for $AUS 200 a month. Christ, that was a fortune, but it was all right, we would be able to live on that. And, when we left, I didn't have a job to go to. I'd looked at getting into the Police in Australia, but they told me I was too old. I wasn't, but I didn't pursue it.

We hired a car and left from Southampton. There was chaos going on in my head. I was thinking about my family. *Are we making a big mistake?* I thought. But I guess it was a bit late to be thinking that.

We travelled to Australia on a ship called Britannis, a Greek boat.

On the ship, there was a telegram and a bunch of flowers waiting for us. It was from my sister and said, 'Bon Voyage.'

Oh my God, I thought. *Should we turn back?* But it was too late and we couldn't do that. Ruth was happy to go, largely because of the problems with her sister and her parent's house. I was in my thirties. It was good to have Ruth with me, although going on a ship was no problem for me.

It was a horrible ship. I reckon it was specifically for immigrants from Britain. It had about twenty million people on board, I reckon. It was unbelievable. Probably, in truth, it was nearer five hundred, but it was crowded. The ship had been restructured. All the cabins had been cut down and cut down and turned from one cabin into three. It was appalling. It was an immigrant ship.

The trip took about six weeks. We didn't go through the Panama Canal, but the other way. Down and round, left, through the Cape of Good Hope. Not Cape Horn, though I could tell you other stories about that one. My grandad was on the windjammers. He went on four month trips, but I'm digressing and I'll get the story muddled. Anyway, as I said, the ship was horrible and we had problems with the food and the staff. The waiters were rude and ignorant. We had a row with one. I could have thrown him overboard.

You get to know people at your table, of course, and learn about where they're going and why. It's not very private. There were twelve of us. Well, this Greek boy was serving us and he just banged the food down on the table. One bloke asked him if he was all right. He was crying one day. He obviously didn't want to be there. To be honest, they all seemed unhappy, but we seemed to have the worst one. We tried to cheer him up a bit and told him if he looked after us a bit better we'd give him a tip. He did in the end. We asked him why he was on the ship and he said he had to be. But we talked to the people at the table too, who were from all over the world. One chap had left a factory job and was going to another one in Sydney. He was a nice guy. I was the only Welshman on the table. Everyone was going to different destinations. Not everyone stayed though. Some didn't like it and went back. One chap wrote to us. He'd gone back because he couldn't sell his house. He was from Hull.

My son got into a few scrapes on the ship. I couldn't stop him. He was on the dance floor and singing. He kept disappearing too. He was only about six and it was slightly worrying because a ship can be pretty dangerous.

In the evenings, there was a French concert pianist called Jean Pierre. A woman called Rosine used to stand beside him to turn the pages for him. He was brilliant. He would often chat to me and I got to know him quite well. Later on, Ruth had to translate his French qualifications into English, before he could get a job. I remember him playing one night and he got a bit cross. Rosine had turned the wrong page, and the ship was rolling about a bit. On one of our stops, he went ashore and was late getting back. If I remember correctly, the pilot had to go and pick him up. He was carrying loads of stuff with him when he returned, like spear guns. Some people were quite upset about this.

'What are you upset for? He's only delayed us by about an hour,' I said.

We stopped in the Canary Islands and South Africa. I thought that was a nice place to stop. When we got to Australia we stopped at Perth first as some passengers were getting off there. Eventually, after about six weeks, we got to our destination: Sydney.

On arrival, Ruth had to see Mr Wolf in Brisbane about her employment. He was the chap who'd organised it all. We travelled up the coast on an open train with wooden seats. It was quite exciting. I was with my family and enjoying it. On the other hand, Ruth had a job to go to, but I was unemployed. Mr Wolf confirmed Ruth's job, that she was highly qualified, that all her papers were there, and that she would be paid a salary of $200.

We took lots of our furniture with us, but it doesn't necessarily travel with you on the same ship. They turn up and they pack up the entire house and take it away on a van. There's a name for it. I can't remember it. But they move it into storage ready to be shipped to foreign parts. We were told it would be delivered to Australia and we'd be reunited with it there. That all worked fine.

Chapter Eleven
Starting a Life in Australia

Near Brisbane, we were put up in huts at a place called Wacol. It was horrible. There was every nationality there. It was a bit like an army camp, but I guess you have to start somewhere. It was outside Brisbane. It was very hot and mosquitoes were biting us. To be honest, my enthusiasm had worn off a bit at that point. Anyway, Ruth was working a temporary job in Ipswich and I was driving her there every morning. I'd gone into town and bought a car for $395, a Ford Zephyr Zodiac. It was small, but it did the job. I paid for it, jumped in and drove it off, with no insurance, no tax and no driving licence! Fortunately, they didn't care.

They're very laid back in Australia. We were on first-name terms straight away. Mr Wolf was a nice bloke, a lovely guy. He said I'd got a bit of a chequered history, job-wise, and asked me what I might do. I thought, with Ruth's salary, that I maybe wouldn't have to work! I was apparently too old to join the police; at least they thought I was. There were many factories up there, but I didn't fancy that.

By chance, I met a guy at Wacol who worked in the prison service and he said they were recruiting up in Townsville. Mr Wolf helped me with this and I ended up training to be a prison officer. I ended up doing weapons training and learning all the prison procedures, which were very complicated.

So, we both had jobs to go to. Now, we needed somewhere to live. Ruth wanted somewhere that wasn't like London. Her job was to be at Pimlico State High School. We ended up choosing Townsville, which is up in the north of Queensland, quite a long way away on the map.

In the evenings, in Wacol Camp, we'd often hang around with the other nationalities. I remember we were once sitting in a big room one night, all talking in different languages. There was this French chap, called Claude. He was a plumber.

He looked at me very intently and said, 'Robert, you speak the English so good, very well.'

I thought, *Well, I am English. I mean, I'm Welsh.* But anyway, I asked him if he was French?

'Oui,' he replied, to which I said he spoke French very well.

It was similar with others, Spanish and German. It breaks the ice, you see.

Anyway, we had to get up to Townsville and find somewhere to live.

I drove all the way up there. It took a long time. It was maybe a thousand miles up the coast. Three families went up together, but only my car arrived there in one piece. It didn't even hiccup. I took it steady, a steady fifty. The car only had three speeds.

So, first of all, we needed to find a house. We knew Ruth's money would be coming in soon and we had some money from the sale of the house at 2 Vicarage Rd, in St Agnes. I went into the Townsville Society, an Estate Agent. I explained we wanted to buy a house. To begin with they looked at us like dirt and asked if we had any money. He said it wasn't worth his time taking us around town if we didn't have the money. Now, I quite liked this approach and confirmed I wanted him to drive us around town. He agreed, but again asked whether we would be able to get a mortgage. I explained that Ruth had a job as a teacher on a government salary and that I had applied for and got into the Prison Service.

Well, the estate agent jumped out of his seat and shot over to us. As we both had government jobs, he happily drove us around town. It was unbelievable. This bloke was chatting away to us, knowing he had two people with money to spend.

We went to this lovely housing estate with lots of trees, not at all like the grey of Wales. There were fruit trees in the garden. It was lovely and I told him so. The agent replied that the owners were at home, so we could pop in. We drove up there and met the sellers and Ruth said we'd have it. The address was 10 French St, Pimlico. I think Maundsley was the name of the people. Or was Moseley? Anyway, they were going back to Britain. They were fed up.

But we liked it. $3000 was the asking price. Ruth said we'd pay that. They were delighted. The agent took us into the garden and asked us to sign the paperwork. The rest was done in the back of the car really. He said it would be about a week and we'd have the house. It was easy. Different country – different world! We got the house. We'd got the jobs, got the house, and off we went!

The kids went to Hermit Park School. That was good. The food was good too in Australia. Lots of fresh food and it meant we had a good diet. But it was too hot, compared to Britain. We stayed there for four years in all: '73 to '76.

Ruth started work teaching. We'd go into Townsville and everyone would be waving her saying, 'Hello, Mrs Maddocks.' I wasn't very popular then, but she was! As time went on, we got to know people. We went out on the town, had barbecues and life was good, with no money worries… no financial worries at all.

I had a Dodge truck at the time and, although I worked shifts and we didn't always have a lot of time together, on days off we'd all get in the truck and drive north. One day, heading north, near Charters Towers, the truck blew up. We didn't have RAC or AA or anything, but we had dollars in our back pocket. People would stop and help you. One guy asked what the problem was and I explained the truck had just stopped and the engine had probably blown up. He told me not to worry and just park it up. He took me down the pub while a new engine was put in! They were just so laid back.

Chapter Twelve
Working at Townsville Prison

My job was a bit complicated. On my first day, I headed off to the prison in the suburb of Stuart, Townsville. The first person I met was the cook. He was Welsh and from Pembroke. I got on quite well with him and he was there throughout the two years I worked there. In some ways he ran the prison. Food, of course, is very important, and he could point out who the bad prisoners were.

It wasn't long before I got to know the place. There were lifers there. They had a big cell area to themselves, but they could walk outside. They were always very respectful to me and knew things about my life. I was chatting to one who was painting the walls and he knew Ruth worked in the art school as a teacher. He asked me if I would show Ruth his artwork.

I asked the boss, Mr Cullen, who said I could do whatever I liked. They didn't really care. I think it was because I was liked. It makes things easy you see. So I showed Ruth his stuff and she thought he was quite good, but he wasn't going anywhere. When I took it back to him, I told him Ruth had said he had a lot of talent, and he said that that made his day and he would treasure her comments. Of course, well… he's probably still in there.

We used to go into the cells each morning. One man would stand outside with the gun and two would go in. It was all part of the routine and the inmates were generally quite happy with it, but you had to shoot the man if he turned around. I wondered if I'd ever be able to do that. Once out of the cell, you took them down and had to search them. This had to be done from the side, in case they kneed you. They always smelled because they hadn't washed and they'd been sleeping. They're wary and I was the same. You'd pat them down and they'd look at you.

Now, like I said, the cook was good to me. He'd tip me when the prisoners came down the stairs in the morning and say, 'Go for him there, that one on the right.'

So I'd say to the prisoner, 'You took a fork out of the canteen last night. It's in your left shoe. Can I have it now?'

They thought I was some sort of magician, and so when they came down from the cell the next morning, they wouldn't go to me, but to another officer. I couldn't search them because they'd say, 'Don't go to that bastard.' But it made me laugh. It was the same with the TV.

I normally left at 11pm (after a 3pm to 11pm shift). Lights out was at 9.30pm. I'd get them all settled down. But early on, before I knew all the rules, they were watching a John Wayne film. Something like in Alcatraz. Those guys had about a year to go. They were safe, not insane, but they still had to be confined at night. You take your gun off and leave it outside before you go into the TV room. Now, the guy at the end was a real bad one – everybody hated him. His language was unbelievable. He said, 'Come here you. I bet you wouldn't want to come in a fucking cell with me.'

'What would I want to go in a cell with you for?' I said. 'I'm all right. I'm going home in a minute.'

I was winding him up. Anyway, they were watching the film, but it was 9.30pm. One of them asked if they could watch the end of it. I didn't see the problem, so he explained that the governor had said lights out at 9.30pm. I asked him when he thought the film would finish, and he said in about an hour. I didn't see a problem with that, so I told them to carry on. I had taken over, you see. 'Carry on,' I said. They didn't really know what I meant, but they were all sitting there on the benches, so I went and made myself a cup of tea. Well, it got to half past ten, the film finished, and they put themselves to bed. They locked themselves in… *ding, ding, ding.* The message got round quick and the other cell blocks got upset. They'd all had lights out at 9.30pm, while the lights were still blazing in my block. The next week I was in another block and another officer was in charge, and it was back to the old routine, but the third week I said to him that we needed to work together on this. I'd been told by the governor to just carry on, so I did it my way. I told the inmates when to put the lights off and they'd do it. I was only an officer, but that was life and I used to get away with it.

Basically, you can choose to be difficult, or not. There was one man there, ex-military and he used to shout at them all. He was called Winchester. He was very posh and it didn't do to upset him. He didn't last long in the job.

Another time, one of the dormitories had to go out to work. They were all waiting to go, but I hadn't received the instructions and I arrived late. The inmates were telling me, 'Boss, we have to go out.' But I didn't know where they had to go.

This Scottish prison officer, Kennedy, came storming up, shouting and swearing at me.

'Hang on, stop there,' I said.

'Pardon?' he asked.

Stop there,' I repeated. 'Don't come bawling at me.'

Anyway, later on, the prisoners were saying to me, 'Oh, boss, you really told him off.'

They were also happy because they'd had a day off work. They made me a cup of tea and it was nice. Okay, they were prisoners, but they weren't killers, just people.

One bloke told me, 'I shouldn't be in here, you know.'

I said, 'Well, that makes two of us!'

I always remembered that they were sent to prison as a punishment, not *for* a punishment. You've got to bend a bit, otherwise you can't make any headway. The inmates could make life a bloody misery for you. But nobody was ever physical with me. I'd stand there and listen to their problems, you see. Some prison officers didn't get it.

I tell you the prisoners had it easy. One guy was released on a Friday and was back on the Monday. They had football, TV, everything. They were also really well fed. There were a lot of Aboriginals in there and they liked being together in a group, with their mates.

'What's the point of being in town,' one said to me. 'I'll kick a few doors in…'

I told him not to do too much damage. Anyway, he explained he'd be back and I'd asked, 'What do you mean?' He told me there was a card game going on in the prison and he hadn't finished it.

It was a good prison, I suppose. We didn't have big problems. There were lots of small incidents, but the prisoners didn't cause too much fuss, because we were armed. We were told, if any were climbing the walls, to fire one shot over their head and one into their body. Not that the rifles would work, because they were never overhauled. They'd never been used and so probably wouldn't fire. The only time I used the pistol was to shoot a snake. I had to go up the ladder onto a catwalk where it was. It was a brown snake and they're pretty dangerous. I had to shoot him, BANG, straight in his head. I then had to write a report and explain to the chief what had happened. They charged me for the bullet, saying I'd wasted it!

The governor was horrible. He was from Clarke, down in Brisbane. He offered me his job, before I left. He asked me if I wanted to take over. I said no. He offered me the job, because apparently we were living in the posh part of town. I didn't know it was posh. It was just called No. 10, French St. There were doctors and dentists there and me.

And there were some crappy places too. It was in the best part of town, but it was only $3000.

I wasn't getting tired of it, but I thought, *I don't want to be a prison officer all my life, no matter how popular I am.* I hated the shifts too, and I felt I had to move on again. Ruth was still teaching in the high school and she was doing very well.

As I said, on the day that I resigned, I was offered the governor's job. Despite this, I was off like a shot. I went into town thinking, *I'll just do what I can do.* I was good at antique restoring. I don't know why, but I opened a shop. I saw premises for rent in town. At the time it was called Melrose and Fenwick. So, I set up shop in there. The rent wasn't much, but it needed a bit of doing up. They asked me what I was going to do in there and I said I was going to do antiques. They said it wouldn't work.

Chapter Thirteen
Antiques and Art

I left the prison service and opened up the shop. It was called Maddock's Antiques, at 657 Flinders Street.

I went in and decorated it, sorted out the windows, and barricaded it. I had to pay rent to the company next door: Fenwick and somebody. It was $16 a week. I filled it up on the first day with stuff I had at the house. I was always into antiques and we'd brought quite a lot with us when we came to Australia. But then I thought, *I've got to start buying furniture now.* I had some, but I went down to the bank and asked if I could borrow some money. The first bank turned me down, but the next was fine. In the second one the chap mentioned he'd seen my wife the week before and he knew her. He just threw money at us because of Ruth's position in the community. I said I wanted $2,000 to buy a bit of furniture and pay some of the rent up front.

'Hang on,' he said. 'Is that enough?'

I said I didn't really want anymore. He didn't believe antiques would work, but thought second-hand goods would. I said I planned to do both. Anyway, I borrowed the money, and I had some furniture I'd brought over from my old home. I took that into the shop to fill it up a bit. I also started buying rusty old brass beds, head and foot stands, which we sand-blasted and tidied up and set up in a room.

I used to open up at ten in the morning, go and get a

burger and a milkshake from a nearby milk bar, and by the time I got back, there would already be customers outside. They would start nagging me, asking where I'd been. The customers were all women, no men. The women did the shopping, didn't they?

I remember the first customer, Mrs Gill. She walked in and she said she was looking for a brass bed. She asked how much and I said $95. I remember it well. It was the first money we took, and quite a lot of money. She said, she didn't want the other part, the bottom, just the top; the head part. I sold it to her and she said she'd send her husband in to pick it up.

Now, Australian people, some of them, can be very brusque and rude. This bloke came in, about a week later. I was sitting there. He was unimpressed.

'Is it that?' he said. The language was a bit stronger. 'Is it that?! Did she pay for that?'

I said she'd paid $95 and he swore a bit more. I suggested he'd better take it home or he'd be in trouble. I told him it was paid for and if he didn't like it, he could just scrap it. Anyway, he took it away. The women were always okay with me. The men just did what they were told. Things started moving fast. Believe it or not, I got to the end of the week and I didn't have any stock left!

I had the money piled up in dollars. I remember I took it home in a bag. Ruth came home from school and asked how it had gone and I replied that I hadn't got any stock left. I emptied all the money onto the bed... it was amazing!

'Christ,' she said. 'You're going to make a lot more.'

'No,' I said. 'It's just a flash in the pan.'

It wasn't. I started buying pianolas and getting those restored. I'd put an ad in the paper, saying I was looking for them and people would ring up and bring them in. For whatever reason, they'd stopped working, but I could restore them. My friend, the singer from the Britannis, Jean-Pierre Martel, also helped. He repaired some of them for me, at least to get them going. I did all the woodwork. My son used to come into the shop, put the roll in and start pumping away on the pedals, playing ragtime. People would pass in the street, hear it and come in. One woman who came in was a pianist. She saw it was a pianola, switched it off and played it normally, like a piano. She asked me what I wanted for it and I quoted her $1000. It had cost me just $200 to restore it and I'd found out they were asking $900 for them in Sydney, so I based it around that. I sold about ten of those. Honestly, I don't plan these things. It's just me.

There was another antiques business in the town called Speckled Hen. They'd been there for twenty years. I didn't want to tread on their toes too much, but I was so popular. A newspaper agency came to do a story on me. They asked what had made me come to Australia, whether I knew there was another shop down the road, and if I thought my business might upset them. I replied that I had no intention of upsetting them and good luck to them. Sadly, they took offence at this remark.

We sold Victorian lampshades that we ordered from England. These came on a ship in a big container, as well as pieces of furniture that I would restore to new. Things went well and I started going further and further afield to buy stuff.

I was pleased to discover Jean-Pierre Martel and his wife Rosine had ended up in Townsville too. She wanted a job and came to work for me in the shop. I always told her, that if I was away, just sell. You can always take ten per cent off. She was a big success and really, I loved her. I realised I'd been in the wrong job. I'd left the prison service where I'd been on about $22 a week and now I was making about $1000 a week. It was amazing. It wasn't easy, but you just have a go. We were in Australia for about four years after the prison job. I guess I had the antiques for one and a half years. It was all crammed in, but it was successful.

The ex-prisoners used to come there as well. Because they had opal mining there, they'd bring in lumps of rock and slam it on the counter. To me, it was just a piece of rock. I had to take it down to Mrs Chong, the Chinese lady down the road. She would tell me what it was worth and I'd sell it on to her.

A nice policeman came to see me at the shop and asked me where my gun license was, manual or book. I explained I hadn't got one and he asked why not. He explained that I was a licensed gun dealer. If you were an antique dealer, you were a licensed gun dealer as well. I was surprised, but he said if I filled out the form he had with him, I could sell guns now too. So I started selling Winchesters. People were bringing them in. It was like the Wild West. They'd come in. I'd pay $50 for a Winchester, 32 and 38 calibres. One bloke came in with a pistol. I had a safe for them all, well not the Winchesters, but for the other guns, and they were selling like hotcakes. I also ordered them from a place in Florida – Arms and Armour Florida it was called. I just looked them up in a big book. The price was good, so it was worthwhile. I did wonder if they'd ever actually arrive, but they did.

We got some swords in once. They weren't Samurai swords, but they looked the part. I put them on display in the window, at night and left the light on. When I opened in the morning I could see the marks on the pane of glass, where people's noses had been pressed up against it. Once I had a phone call about one of the swords at 7.30pm at home. The guy said he had to have it and asked me to come to the store there and then. I didn't mind. It was a nice evening. He paid cash, all dollars, no cheques and I went to the pub afterwards. They weren't rare as such, but they were nice pieces, probably reproductions, I don't know. But they looked good.

I got a cannon from a place that was closing down. It had been made by the Winchester Repeating Arms

Company. I sold it to an ex-military guy and he used to fire it in the mornings. Boom!

I used to go to a place called Charters Towers, an old gold mining town, about sixty miles from Townsville. Now driving out there, back in my day, you might see one other car. It was a very different way of life. If you saw someone broken down, you would stop though.

I was ploughing along and I saw this chap changing a wheel. I pulled over to help. I asked him if he was okay and he told me to sod off! I could see his spare tyre was in even worse condition than the one he was replacing. I watched him do it, but he told me again to sod off. Okay, so I drove off. I was going along about 50mph when, *Whoosh,* he went flying past me. He was heading for Charters Towers. It was like the American West.

Heading into the bigger towns, the first thing you'd come to was the pub. You walk in and they'd put a pint on the bar for you, like a John Wayne movie. Mind you, it was so bloody hot, you'd pour that first ice-cold beer over your head sometimes. It was such a relaxed life. You put $20 on the bar and they'd keep refilling you. And you would drive home afterwards. You wouldn't hit anybody because there was nobody around. It was too hot. Nobody was out for a stroll! Ruth often said the heat was too much.

One day, in Charters Towers, I went to visit a gunsmith who worked there. He was retired and lived in a caravan beside the river. People were telling me that the guns I was buying were damaged or worn, the springs not working, etc. So, I took a load to this guy. I forget his name, but he was a very elderly gentleman with a beard. He was sitting by the river and was panning. Making about $50 a day he was.

'Come here Robert and I'll show you what to do,' he said. 'It's very easy.'

He took the gun apart in front of me and explained that the Winchester Repeating Arms Company would take a gun off the production line, one in every few hundred, and break it down completely, like a car. They'd re-do it, polish it and reassemble it. He said, if I had one of those, maybe one in every five hundred, I'd be a millionaire. It's the difference between owning a Ford car, or a Rolls Royce. When he'd reassembled it he said, 'Feel that.' It was a beautiful gun. He asked what I'd paid for it and I said about $50. He told me it was now worth $500. I sold it on, but what an amazing thing that was… a gunsmith, in those days, sitting by the river, enjoying himself.

At the same time, there was an auction going on in Charters Towers, which interested Ruth. It was a hot, scorching day and the auction was selling antiques and paintings. Ruth was happy in Australia, although she didn't like the kids. She liked the teaching job though. She was tough in her own way; very academic and knowledgeable. Amazingly, she put up with me.

At this auction, there was a painting on the floor by the entrance. I was going to move on fairly rapidly, but Ruth said, 'Bob, that painting there is from 1872. It's not very old, but it's by Sebastian Hirst. He was a painter who travelled around. You could call him itinerant.'

I didn't know who he was. Apparently, he was on laudanum – or whatever they used to keep them going – but he was pretty drugged up, I think. But he was good if a very naïve painter. He might paint a horse and a man, the man bigger than the horse. It was all a bit weird, the perspective was all out. It was horrible, but Ruth said, 'We're going to buy it.' The auctioneer wanted to move on quickly, but Ruth called him back. He said it would be $20. We bought it, but left some of his other drawings, not knowing they were valuable.

Anyway, we took this painting home and we had it for thirty years. Then, maybe we were struggling a bit, or needed money for something, but we decided to sell it. So, my son, who was going around Australia on a tour for six months, took a photo of it with him. He went to a museum in

Canberra, where they were aware of Ruth and her having worked up in Townsville and enquired about this painting, which they had a copy of in that museum. My son told them that his mum still had the real one and that it remained in good condition. Paperwork was drawn up and sent to us over the Internet and they offered us $23,000. It was probably worth more, but Ruth was satisfied that the offer was enough, and that the painting should go back to the museum. It's there now, with her name on it. You can see it if you go to the museum in Canberra. They told us when they received it that it was better than they had expected. That was because Ruth had kept it in a darkened area and the colours were still beautiful.

I said to Ruth, 'You're bloody clever, you are. I didn't like it, did I?'

I still don't. It cost us $20. Anyway, it's gone. But they gave us a copy.

Chapter Fourteen
Leaving Australia

Anyway, after four years, it was the heat that finally made us decide to come back. Ruth couldn't cope with it any more. It was always hot, in the car, on the seats, everywhere. I asked her if she was sure and she said she was. And, of course, her parents were back there. It does tug a bit you see, when there are parents and grandparents back home. Was my father still alive then? I'm not sure. Yes, I think he was.

Oh, I didn't mention it. Before I left the Prison I'd looked at a job in the government; in immigration, in Sydney. They wanted a person who'd been to sea, had been in the police force and was trained in firearms. The job was for someone on the docks, to go onto the ships, looking for people... immigrants, drugs, contraband, I don't know. But it took them seven months to do all their checks, going back all through my life, even to my school. When they went to my father's house in Tennyson Rd, they were met by a man who said, 'Fuck Off' to them. How do you go forward in your life with that? I'd had the same when I went for the police force. Despite this, I got the job, but the news came too late. Ruth said I should have taken the job. Although it was based in Sydney, I'd have been moving around a lot, visiting every port.

We sold Maddocks Antiques and we booked a passage

back on a ship. That meant getting down to Sydney again. I had to clear out the stock, which was bloody awful in that heat. I employed two men from the local labour exchange. We had two forty-foot containers all loaded up with furniture. It was amazing, but we filled them, stuck them on a trailer and left them at the docks. That lot all went down to Sydney by sea, but we drove down in the car.

By the time we got there, I was tired. The kids were tired and angry and we had to feed them. So I said to Ruth that we'd get ourselves into a hotel and book a ship. And we hadn't sold stuff in the containers either yet. They would be sold at auction in Sydney. That's why we took them there. We had to stay there until the stuff had been sold, and then book a ship back. We didn't know how regular the ships were, but I knew there wouldn't be one every day.

I discovered that there was a ship in port, the Taras Shevchenko, which was going back to Southampton in one week. I wondered if we could make it, but I booked it, paid for it in cash and said we'd be there. The auction was due the same day that it was due to depart.

Meanwhile, we were in this hotel. It wasn't a normal hotel. It was full of odd people. It was definitely cheap, so I booked it. One bloke came down one morning while we were having breakfast. He was banging around there, throwing the food around, saying, 'She's onto me. She's onto me again.'

The lady in charge was a bit of a mental case. She used to shout at him. She said to the guy, 'Go upstairs and clean the bloody windows.'

We were in our bedroom and he was on a ladder outside. He was tapping at the window and banging it, so we opened it and I asked if he was all right. He was sort of hanging on and said he didn't like the height. I had to pull him in! Then she came looking for him. I said to Ruth it was all a bit crazy, but we had to get out of there that day anyway.

But then we couldn't find our son, who was about nine

or ten. There were all these toilets on the ground floor and the landlady was yelling his name. I was standing back because she was shouting so loud. A little voice said, 'I'm not Julian' and it wasn't because Julian was in another one.

Later, we got down to the auction room. The auctioneer was called Fred Reece, a lovely guy.

He said, 'Christ Bob, what time is your boat?

I said about 6.30pm. Fred said they'd got everything lined up ready, but they had five hundred lots to get through. I asked if he could help me out. It was 2.30pm and I didn't think we'd get through. We'd made about $12,000 that day and Fred asked if that was enough. I said it was because I had to go. He asked for an address to forward the cheque to me, but I wasn't sure which address to give. Cardiff was my home town, so I knew Nat West was there and suggested he look them up and send the money to them there. He did it. It all went through and there was no problem.

But I was in a bit of a panic when I got on the ship, as we had two vehicles to get on, the Zephyr and the pick-up truck, a Ute. So I looked around and saw a stevedore. I approached him and asked him if he wanted a car. I couldn't take both on board, so had to decide between the Zephyr and the truck. The truck was handier and that was full of our stuff too. So, ridiculous as it was, I just gave the guy the keys to the car. I've still got a picture of that car. He was happy and off he went, the ship honking away, getting ready to depart.

We got the truck up into the ship, which was all paid for and then I had a look around. It was a lovely ship and the Russians were lovely people, very polite and speaking broken English. Our cabin was 315. Going out we'd had 513! There were thousands of cabins anyway and over a hundred crew, but maybe only a hundred or so passengers. It couldn't have been running at a profit, but it was beautiful.

We moved off and this time we went the other way, via the Panama Canal, across the Pacific, by Hawaii and across the Atlantic, to dock in Southampton. It was a lovely trip. I couldn't do it again; you need a lot of energy. I'm tired of just thinking about it now.

I've got all the pictures of the ship: pictures of my wife sitting there, having breakfast. When you board you give them your passports, so they know when your birthdays are. We had both our birthdays on that ship: 2nd and 9th March, a week between each other. They gave us a cake, it was great. I said thank you. We were sat there, being waited on by a lady who was singing to us, and we talked with her about Russia, in her broken English. Other people were looking at us, probably wondering why they didn't have a cake. One bloke, from Cardiff, asked me about it. I told him I got cake all the time, even though I asked them not to. That was on Ruth's birthday and I knew there might be no more cake coming you see. It was just a joke. Next week, I got a cake. I told him I'd asked them not to, and asked him when his birthday was. He said it was in December.

'You won't be getting any cake,' I said.

During the weeks on a ship, you got to know the crew. This Russian lady liked us and very popular I was. Anyway, she said, while we were in Panama, 'We can't leave or jump ship, because our people will be… taken out.'

I thought, *Really! How lucky we are.* They all thought about jumping off at Panama. They couldn't because their parents would be targeted by the authorities back in Russia.

Anyway, it was brilliant. We went through Panama. I've been through Panama three times. I know it intimately: The Panama Canal and Gatun Locks. It's fabulous what they did there you know, the Americans. And I'll tell you what…. the first time you go to sea for a long time, the scent of land… Africa and Panama. You start to see bits of leaves and trees coming down and you know you're getting nearer land. The smell gets better and better. It's like being a castaway.

We got back in June. I left all my superannuation there. I haven't been paid out. They can't find me now. I've got an accountant on it now. I've got $5000, maybe more, but they can't find me. If I owed them money. I'm sure they'd find me.

Chapter Fifteen
Home on the Range: Cornwall Part II

1976 – 1994
'When you have to do it, then it's work, work, work!''

When we got back to Southampton we didn't really know what we were going to do, or where we were going to live. Our initial plan was to head for Cornwall. We were travelling in the pick-up truck we'd brought from Australia. We had all the things that we owned in the world in the back of that truck. As we reached the dock gates there was a policeman there. He stopped me and immediately I knew we were back in Britain. He said, 'I should get those tyres done.'

I wasn't really in the mood for that and told him I was in a hurry. Well, he wasn't impressed. I just wasn't in the mood for it. I'd been a police officer and I was just trying to re-enter Britain. They've got no idea and they wind you right up. I told him I'd get all the tyres done. They were massive tyres you know. Then he started asking about the tax. Well, it was under Australian Tax and I knew that covered me for twelve months, which he should have known. But he didn't. He'd had no idea. I didn't want to overdo it and knew I had to be respectful, so I said, 'I think you'll find, officer, that the tax covers me for twelve months.'

I suggested he could check with his superiors. He didn't like that. He asked me for my address. I replied that I didn't have an address. I was getting upset then. I just wanted to get off the docks.

I explained to him that we'd just come back home. He wanted to know where we were going, so I said we were going back to Cornwall, where Ruth's parents still were. It was a target to head for, although I wasn't sure where we were going to end up. I could have said Cardiff, but we were going to Cornwall. We eventually set off, after chatting him up a bit to get rid of him.

We stopped en route at a hotel, well a pub, in Devon. It's gone now. It was in Honiton, a small local pub, offering Bed & Breakfast. I parked the truck at the back of the pub, had a meal and a bath. Ruth was stressed and said we should have stayed in Australia! I thought, *Here we go*, but I said we could always go back.

We eventually got down to Cornwall. We stayed with Ruth's parents at first, at Mt Hawk. We had nowhere else to go. They owned the property again and Barbara was no longer living there. I did odd jobs initially, like cheese packing in Camelford. I was only there for about a month. It was a horrible, stinking job. I also did some car insurance sales for a guy called Captain Hunter, who had his offices in Porthtowan. I'd just got talking to him and he asked me what I was doing and gave me a job. I worked for him while we were staying at Mrs Chapman's. I sat in the office and made phone calls. I used to go to the pub with him too. Those were hard times, the first six months or so back in the UK. I couldn't afford to buy a house with the money I was earning. Ruth was asking if maybe we should book a trip back to Australia. I was getting a bit tetchy and suggested she give me a break.

We went down to the coast one day into Truro, where we knew the area. I said we had to get somewhere to rent or buy. We had some cash in the bank, as the money had been sent from the auction. It kept coming from Australia in bits and pieces, as they sold the rest, but it all came eventually.

In Truro, we found an estate agent. It was an ancient old place in Camelford, with curled-up pictures on the walls. They were selling an interesting seventeenth-century derelict farmhouse. They were asking £7,000 for it. I thought that would do me, and we had some money in the bank. Ruth, very bluntly, said, 'If we don't get this house, we're going back.'

Anyway, we arranged to view the property. The agent didn't come with us, but we found the place. Ruth actually fell in love with it, even though it hardly had a roof on, there was a dodgy water supply and no sewerage. It was ancient, with oak beams and big fireplaces. Ruth said I could do all the work needed. She knew I could. I'm very good, you see. I can build you a house, no sweat, though not the electrics and the plumbing. I don't know: it came from somewhere. It also came with nine acres of land, running down to the river Ottery, and we were sold on that! We saw the place and we had to buy it.

We bought it from two blokes: Preller and Ward. One was a farmer and one was a businessman. They couldn't sell the property to anyone else, but they saw this idiot turn up and suggested we could do a deal. I told them I had £7000 and no more and that I wanted to buy the house that day, or I was going back to Australia. They said not to worry and we could sort it out. Mr Ward was nice. He could see I was stressed and he invited us up to the farmhouse for a meal. Thinking quickly on my feet, I said, 'We're having it.' I maybe shouldn't have been so quick, but we were stuck. The sellers agreed our price. The solicitors who acted for me were quite good and I got a small mortgage: £2,000, from somebody in Launceston.

Our neighbour, another farmer, was a Mr May. He kept

cows on a seventy-acre farm and had milking parlours. That caused another problem, which we'll get to later on.

We began living in a caravan. It had water, but as for sewerage, we had to be boy scouts and, before we got the septic tank put in, which we did, we had to just dig a trench. It was a bit crazy and we had to get something happening. I had to find work fast and thought, *What can I do to get money in?*

I said to Ruth, 'You stay here and I'll go and get some money.'

I went to work then in a chicken factory and I also went back up to Penarth at weekends and took a job in a pub, The Pilot Hotel. I can't believe it now, but there was more work there than down in Cornwall. There was nothing in Cornwall.

At that time, my sister got in touch and told me that my father had died and had left me £3,000, which she had kept for me. She hadn't realised I was back in the country, but my sister was lovely and we got on famously. I explained to her what was happening and where I was working. I was going back and forth each weekend. I was very tired, but I was earning good money. I knew The Pilot Hotel and all the people in there. The owner was a Scotsman, Mc-something. He was a bit tetchy with me, but I stuck it out for about five months. It paid for a lot of work that needed doing down in Cornwall.

One day, I came out of the pub and I saw this sign, offering a property for sale at No 2 John Street. Unbelievable. It was another derelict home. They wanted £7,000 for it. I told Ruth. Why I bought it, I don't know, but I got on the phone with a solicitor, a Mrs Davies, who knew me, and asked about it. She explained that the mortgagee was in possession. There was only £3,000 left due on the mortgage. The asking price was £7,000, but the mortgagee wanted only £3,000, to clear the debt. The poor beggar was in prison, which was his bad luck, so I bought it, for cash, with all I had. I didn't have the solicitor's fee, but I was still working in the pub. I got the money from my sister and bought it.

A week later, this woman came into the pub and said hello to me. She and her husband were retiring from the Clive Arms Public House on the same street, opposite John Street. She asked me if I wanted to sell the house. I'd only just bought it. They had the deeds to The Clive Arms and proposed that we might do a straight swap. I probably should have said yes, but I said no, because I didn't have a clue or any interest in running a pub, and my home was in Cornwall. I said no, anyway.

At first, I rented out John Street to students to get some additional income. It was £4 a week. I suppose in those days it might have been better to tart it up and sell it, but things overtake you. I was working in the pub and earning money, had a home with Ruth in Cornwall and had no mortgage on the St John's Street property. I felt like a life with no mortgage was living like a king. But renting was no good. Things didn't go so well with the students and they were messing about, abusing the place and seeking the council's help to try and get the rent adjusted. They were all at Cardiff University. I'd never have them again. They were all foreigners. One was from Venezuela, one was from Chile, and they were very aggressive too.

But, because I was local, I had some contacts. One was a police officer, Clive and another Irish chap, Dick, who knew me. He said the students shouldn't abuse me and he'd come down there with me. We went in and saw they were stealing electricity – which was quite a crime – and that there were more people in the house than there should have been. I didn't have to do any talking, because Dick spoke to them, told them his name and mine and that if they abused me, he was going to throw them out of the house there and then. They said they'd call the police, but I knew my mate Clive was coming there later and he was on my side. Today, of course, you have to be much more careful – you can't just throw them out. But you also can't have bad people. We got some out, but one of them wanted to argue. I found out later from Clive, that one of them was wanted on a warrant. He said to that guy, 'I've come down here to check there's been no breach of the peace, but you shouldn't be here. You're wanted on a warrant.'

So he took him away and that was another one gone. After that, the others left too. They didn't like the police coming around, you see. They probably had drugs there. Anyway, very shortly after, we'd got them out.

I'd played with Clive in the street in Penarth when we were boys. We thought he lived there with his parents, but it turned out it was his aunt and uncle. He just preferred to be with them, rather than his parents in Cardiff. I got on with his father, who was himself a police sergeant. He said to me one day that I'd got more sense than all the other kids. Maybe I did have, but I was so shy then. Not now, of course. I sing now, karaoke, in the pub and I enjoy it and they all laugh. I didn't get into the police in Wales though, did I? But Clive did, of course. He breezed in. He came in the pub one day after, claiming he'd got in on his own merits, but I always thought if my father had been a sergeant, I'd have got in too.

As it was, I didn't like my father and he didn't like me. My sister told me my mother was terrified of him and I knew that it was always panic stations whenever he was coming. That was our situation. Other families seemed more normal, playing football together or maybe going swimming together, but not mine. That's life. Clive and I drifted apart over the years. I think he's still alive, somewhere out near Dinys Powys I think. He might be dead. It's just childhood memories. I wonder sometimes about the kids in my school. Were they successful? You always think they must be doing better than you.

Anyway, I sold the house in John Street to a gentleman

who came into the pub. He asked me what I'd paid for it, but I told him that wasn't his business. He'd seen it up for sale before but had missed his chance when I bought it. He offered me £13,000 cash for it and I thought, *From three to thirteen thousand isn't bad, is it?* Well, I didn't have any money. I thought I'd won the Pools. I said I'd give it some thought, but then quickly said, 'Yes.' So, I had £13,000 in the bank then. I went back to Cornwall and told Ruth I didn't have to keep going back to Wales for work, as we'd got some money in the bank now.

When we'd bought Old Newham, I thought the water wasn't going to be a problem, because there was a tap in an out-house, but the first time I turned it on it hissed a bit and the water came out that was black.

I bought a tractor and went up to the garage in the village, about half a mile and brought water back in a drum. So that was sorted for now. And with the money I had, I got a chap in to build us a sceptic tank, which was important to get a working toilet. Imagine how wonderful that was: water and a septic tank.

We were still living in the caravan. I'd work until maybe 3.30am, doing the house: the carpentry, putting in new beams, and I was still working at the chicken factory to have a bit of money coming in. I was so busy, but I was fit then. When you have to do it, then it's work, work, work.

My daughter annoyed me. I'd get back in the caravan, maybe 2.30am for a wash. There was no water left because she'd used it all up. Both the children were going to school in Launceston then, and I went in there one day and got myself arrested. This was still in 1977. And I was still driving my Ute with Queensland, QLD plates PPE 499. I was still using it because I was selling scrap on top of everything else. I got it from the farm, loads of stuff that had just been left there over the years. I was busy making money. It was chaos. The scrap didn't make much, but that's how it was.

One day, I was delivering scrap over Bodmin, and the

road there was very steep. I was at the top and came down the hill, heading for this scrap place. I had about two tons of scrap behind me. I put the brake on and heard a big bang. Ruth was with me and I told her not to panic, but we were going down faster now, with no brakes. So I was trying to change gears and use the handbrake. I realised that if we carried on down the hill, we'd be dead. I saw this big entrance to a place, with big pillars, like an embassy. There was a man out front in a uniform. I thought, *I'll have to turn in there, because I've nowhere else to go.* I managed to turn in, but one of the wheels was wobbling now. This chap tried to stop me, but had to leap out of the way. I rolled into the forecourt of the place, rammed the truck up against the wall and the wheel fell off. He came storming up to me and asked if I knew this was the residence of so and so. I told him he'd nearly lost his life trying to stop me entering and he replied that he was calling the police. They eventually turned up, but there wasn't much they could do. It was clearly an accident. The brakes had failed. All they concluded was that I might want to take both the truck and the scrap to the scrap merchants. In the end, they took it all away and, as it had been a bad day, we said never again. I think I got a cheap car later.

But it was before that, that the officer stopped me in the street in Launceston. I told him that my children were in school there. He replied that they couldn't be, because we'd just got off a ship! I said we'd left the ship a few months before, but he thought I was just trying to be clever. I tried to engage solicitors: Parnell, Godwin & Chegwin, but they were retained by the police, so that was no good, as there was a conflict of interest – and it wouldn't be the last time that happened.

Anyway, the police arrested me because there was another chap, driving a truck like mine. His name was John Green and he'd been going around the place, booking into hotels and then disappearing, without paying. So, he was wanted for fraud. They thought my truck was his. It was very similar. You can't make it up, can you? They thought they had me. I offered the policeman my passport. He snatched it off me. Ruth was with me and getting upset. I again tried to explain that we had come off the ship some time ago, but he wouldn't have it and arrested me.

We drove off down the street in Launceston, one police car in front, one behind and me in the middle. I was waving at people, because they all knew me, you see. The policeman asked me how I knew everyone and I said it was because I lived there! He didn't think that could be right. I told him he was making a mistake and they had got the wrong guy. We sorted it out when we got back to the police station and they realised their mistake.

Now, because I got off, the one policeman got quite upset, I don't know why. But he kept following me around for the next four to five weeks. Every time I parked somewhere, he'd appear. One day, while I was shopping, he stopped me again. It was getting quite silly and more personal. I was parked, stationary, getting some petrol. He came up behind me in his patrol car, approached me and said he was checking my tyres. I hadn't checked them for a while. They were very wide tyres and I guess they had some bald patches. Anyway, he wanted to get me on something, carried out a cursory examination and claimed the tyres were seventy per cent worn.

In court later, he claimed he'd examined the whole circumference of the wheel, but the truck had been stationary. The judge queried this, that the truck was stationary and that he couldn't have examined the bottom. The police officer claimed he hadn't had to, because he could see from the rest that the tyres were no good. He got told off for that, but the judge then said that we'd just ignore that.

Anyhow, I got fined £100. I didn't have the money, but not paying risked going to Exeter Prison. The magistrate asked me about it and I said I wasn't paying. She asked me why and I said the police officer had overreacted based on a personal grudge. It was personal and when I left the dock he came round, put the cuffs on me and forced me down the stairs, but at the waiting police car he was told to take the cuffs off. The magistrate tried to persuade me to just pay the fine, but I thought it was all wrong. I was objecting to a technicality, I know that, but I just felt it was all wrong. I was being stubborn. I could have found the money, but when you're short of money, well... you know.

The magistrate was quite upset and so were the police officers in the car. They knew the officer who'd arrested me – his name was Robert too – and they knew he'd made it personal. In the car, they took the cuffs off and explained they were going to take me to Exeter Prison. I said, 'Carry on.'

I actually spent the first night in the local cells and went up to the prison the next day. I was given a ten-day sentence, but I quite enjoyed it! I felt like the country singer, Johnny Cash. You all walk around in a kind of circle; it's exercise. I was walking around, singing this song, thinking I'd walk the line. And I knew the system, because I'd been in it before, hadn't I? I tried them all out: police officer, prison officer... then a prisoner. Obviously, I didn't mention in prison that I'd been a police officer. Now, I'm a pensioner: it's all the 'P's in my life. Johnny Cash was in prison too; a lot of these famous people have dodgy backgrounds. It just happens, doesn't it?

I'm a chatterbox. I got to know a guy in there. He was doing three months. I shared a cell with him. Latchford his name was. The prison was pretty foul. You have to slop out in the morning and the toilets are awful. I didn't really mind that, but when you're in a room with another man, locked up, you don't know what he's like, do you? He used to mutter in his sleep. I was in the top bunk and he was on the bottom. I didn't sleep much. I used to stay alert. Anyway, the ten days were quite uneventful and I got on with him okay. He couldn't read or write and I used to help him out. He did ask about my background and I covered quite a lot, but I never mentioned having been a police officer. I told him I'd been in the Merchant Navy, which he thought was interesting. The conversations went round and round. You're locked up twenty hours a day, so you've got to pass the time.

I had ten days to do, but I came out after eight for good behaviour! I got a bus back to Camelford. Ruth didn't know I was coming home. I just appeared.

Anyway, I got over all that and back to life at Old Newham. I was working on all that, getting it all going, fixing up the house, when suddenly the bank manager came around asking me if I wanted any more money. He said they had a new programme where they were offering loans for investment in agriculture. I was unsure, but he asked whether I'd considered chicken farming. I hadn't. He mentioned I'd got nine acres of land with the property and a few barns on the land, plus there was a packing station locally in Camelford, which would take all the eggs. He convinced me that it might be a good idea. Now, I'm not a farmer, and there'd be lots of chickens laying eggs.

I ended up with seven hundred chickens. In those days the approach was called 'Deep Litter'. The chickens would be locked in a barn at night and come out in the morning into a fenced area, where the foxes couldn't get them. They feed on the grass. We had a lot of land there. They weren't in cages and could more or less go where they wanted. What we call free range nowadays.

So I got the chickens in and they were laying like hell and, for the time being, I was quite happy, making a small profit. I bought a minivan and took the eggs down to a Camelford packing station. It was going good. They were happy to take them all: large or small or oddly-shaped. This went on for three to four months. We were doing quite well, making a profit and paying off the loan. Then suddenly, the next time I went, the packing station guy told me they were closing down.

It was a few years after we'd joined the Common Market and they had to introduce an upgraded packing system, so the eggs could comply with the EU directive. Well, there you are – they couldn't do small, medium and large anymore, but had to do 1, 2, 3, 4, etc. with no bumps in them, no discolourations, and they couldn't afford to recalibrate all the machines.

I said, 'It's madness. What happens to me now?'

He could only say sorry. I had seven hundred chickens, laying eggs, with nowhere to sell them. There was a panic then. The bank manager wasn't happy when I told him I couldn't carry on because they'd closed the packing station down. We started selling them off at the roadside then, but there's only so many you can sell. We were eating eggs every day and the chickens started dying off. I wasn't a farmer, was I? Another farmer took some, just to help me out. Sometimes, when they roost at night in a corner of the barn. One would lie down, and then another would lie on top of it and another and so on. You could open it up in the morning and in that pile, some would be dead, suffocated. That happened more or less every day. We got through it eventually and got rid of that problem. I told Ruth I couldn't keep on like this and she said, 'We won't do chickens again, will we?'

I said, 'No!'

We'd got the house nicely done up. I rebuilt it, put the beams up by myself and put in stone fireplaces. When Mr Ward came down, the farmer I'd bought it off, he nearly passed out. He had thought it couldn't be brought back from where it was and said he wished he'd never sold it to me. I said it was too late! He was a nice guy though.

But we had another problem at Newham. The water suddenly stopped coming through. It came by gravity from a big reservoir, up above us, on Mr May's farm. Pipes ran from there, under the ground, to us. It had been sluggish at first because it hadn't been used for so long, but it had been getting better, and then suddenly it stopped completely. A chap came round to look at it and said that My May, who did milking had dug up the fields, going down nine feet, and in the process, the clay pipes bringing the water to me had been broken. Well, they were only four feet down.

I went to see him. He was upset and I was upset. I told him he'd cut off my water. He said he needed more for his cows! The machine was amazing; chomping down and laying these new pipes. However, because he'd gone down so low with the new pipes, they couldn't pick up the water from my reservoir.

Anyway, he said he'd put in new pipes, eight feet down, and another tank, and provide a pump to get the water to me. I wasn't happy at the idea of pumping water up from a container and the whole thing didn't work out very well. I needed an electricity supply to make a pump work and that was going to cost me a lot of money. It also transpired that the firm of solicitors dealing with this: Parnell, Godwin and Chegwin, were acting for both of us – another conflict of interest. I could have sued the pants off them, but I didn't. I'm just a normal guy, Ruth wasn't settled and she was saying she wanted to go back to Wales. I felt the same way, after the chicken fiasco and now the water problems, but I said we had to think carefully, as the kids were in school and settled there. But I decided to sell. I panicked a bit, you see.

But someone came down and bought the house for £50,000. I'd paid £9,000 for it, so we made a bit. He had a Rolls Royce this guy, very posh. I did tell him about the water problem. He wasn't worried about that. He said he'd have mains water put in from the main road. He did exactly that. See, he had money whereas I'd never had much. Well, we'd got some now, maybe £38,000. I'd rebuilt the place:

new stone and new roofs, beams, flagstones. And it looked amazing. And there were two barns – where the chickens used to be, but they'd gone. He applied for planning permission and he got it – for another three-bedroom house. That was all right. I was off, and I felt like I wanted to go back to Wales, where I'd feel a bit safer.

Chapter Sixteen
College Farm, Carmarthenshire

So off we go again. I was quite familiar with Carmarthen and soon spotted an advert in the paper for a property near Newcastle Emlyn. It was being sold at auction. It was another seventeenth-century farmhouse, with seventy acres of land.

Fifty acres was grass and the other twenty was woodland and a river. It was called College Farm.

I went up there and stayed in a pub in Spilman Street. The pub's gone now. I stayed overnight. The owner, Euan, knew the area and offered to run me over to the property in his car. This caused a bit of a row with his wife, who complained that he couldn't run off, leaving her to run the pub. He replied that he wouldn't be long. He did some farming himself and he thought the land was good, and that I would be able to rent it out to the local farmers.

I went to the auction. There were many people there. We hadn't got the money from Old Newham yet, although we'd sold it on paper, but we did have the completion date. The auctioneer was Bob Jones, who is no longer with us. He was a Welsh speaker – they all were. I could understand a bit, but I don't speak Welsh. My French is better and that's bad enough. The lot included the farmhouse, with the addition of an old bake house to the side, and the land. I wanted it. The house needed work, but it did have a roof on it.

I set my budget and bid up to £32,000. Unfortunately, it kept going up and then suddenly this bloke said, '£70,000.' Well, of course, I didn't have a chance. Afterwards, Bob Jones, the auctioneer approached me. He knew I'd bid up to £32,000. Then the chap who'd bought it came up to me too. His name was Glyn Davis. He was a nice guy, a Welsh farmer. He apologised for bidding against me and then explained that he was buying the farm because it had previously been his uncle's. He only wanted the fifty acres at the top, which was all grass, for his cattle. I asked about the other twenty-two acres of land. The bit with a wood and a river on it, but he replied that that was no good to him.

Glyn had a daughter called Rachel as well. He was a lovely guy. I watched as Bob and Glyn had a chat. Later, Glyn approached me and offered to sell me the house and the twenty-two acres for £35,000.

He said, 'If you can fence the top and right away down the drive…' which was a mile long, '…we'll put in water for you and give you right of access.'

Again, there was no sewage disposal facility either and, as you can imagine, I was worried about that. I went down to the estate agent with Bob Jones. He said he was acting for Glyn Davies and offered me the property there and then on a handshake. I agreed and paid for it. There was no mortgage.

At the time, I had a very good solicitor, Gwillym Richards; he's dead now too. He was in Newcastle Emlyn in Bridge Street and another lovely guy. He thought I was mad buying College Farm, but he looked after me well. He'd been in The Royal Navy on a supply ship on the Yangtze River in China. This was during the fighting between the communists and the nationalists in 1949. His ship, the Amethyst, was shelled by the communists and very few survived, but one of the survivors, Gwillym told me, was called Maddocks. So there you go.

He was sharp as a needle, but also often in a world of

his own. He was on the top floor, with his secretary, Eva Hope, downstairs. She was a long-suffering girl who really looked after him. Every time I went to see him, I'd climb the stairs and it was always dark in his office. Anyway, I got on quite well with him. I loved the guy. I went to his funeral and there were hundreds there. He was buried facing his office. I've just thought of another story about him. We took on a case against Lloyds Bank, but we'll save that.

Ruth didn't know anything about me buying College Farm. She was still in Cornwall, worried about things down there and getting rid of the remainder of the chickens! I went back and told her all about it. I assured her that I could do the work that was needed, and I mentioned it had a bluebell wood and a river. I was sure she would love it, but obviously she wanted to get up there and see it.

We filled the minivan with lots of our stuff, put some more in storage and went up. Ruth cried when she saw the place and not with tears of joy! She asked me what I thought I'd done and I said, 'Just trust me.' She said she'd heard that before, but she knew I was good with my hands. I promised her we'd stay in the hotel this time and I'd work my back off. I had to.

We stayed at the Boars Head Hotel and I got to work. Unfortunately, in 1980, I had to have an operation to fuse my spine. I was in hospital. Two of us went in on the same day, for a similar operation – the other chap never came back out!

I'd broken my back, probably whilst working in the tin mine for Consolidated Gold Fields. I had a crack in my spine but didn't know it. I might have done it even before that. Possibly when I was working on the new pier in Penarth with G Tate. You may remember I fell and landed on the staging piles. Anyway, just before 1980 I'd been in so much pain. I had to go in and have an operation at Glangwili Hospital, Carmarthen. I forget the surgeon's name, but he was a lovely chap. They rotated me on this thing. They didn't find anything at first, but third time lucky they noticed a crack in my spine. This was what had been causing the problem. So I had the spinal fusion operation, which cured it up to a point, but it also meant I wasn't quite so mobile, particularly when bending down. It's life, isn't it? I've done so many things and some dangerous things, but I've survived, more by luck than judgment. I've still got the problem now at eighty-three. I take tablets to keep it at bay and do exercises. I receive a disability benefit because of it. I started the exercises back in 1980, lying down and rolling left and right, but even back then my muscles were getting progressively weaker.

As you can imagine, I was worried that I wouldn't be able to work on the house. Fortunately, I had some good neighbours. They were Irishmen, two brothers, Mick and Pat McDonnell. So when I got out of the hospital, I discovered that they'd been in and plastered the whole place. I thanked them and gave them a bottle of whisky.

I went to one of their parties once and somebody laced my drink with whisky. Whisky and me don't get on and I'm like Jekyll and Hyde. I was told the next day that I'd gone into a kind of frenzy and had told one of the brother's best friends to f-off and get out of the house. I couldn't believe I'd said that, but they had witnesses. They were doing some renovations in their place, so I think I got a bit confused, thinking I was in my own house. I think they exaggerated a bit, but I had to apologise to everybody who was at that party. No one ever admitted to spiking my drink.

Anyway, after coming out of the hospital, things got going again at College Farm, although it took me seven years to fully renovate the place. I got the bakehouse going first, built a fireplace and had a log fire going. There was plenty of wood down there, of course. It was cosy. I built a staircase and made bunk beds for the kids. This time we had a toilet and running water. It was beautiful – home from home. The kids went to school and I started work on the main house.

It had been a lovely place in its time, owned by an old cattle dealer. I found out he'd been an alcoholic. Strangely, everywhere I went in the building I found bottles of whisky: under the rafters, the beams, and in the outhouses. When people came around, they said I was drinking a lot.

'They're not mine!' I responded.

'Oh, yes, we've heard that before!' they countered.

We had plenty of space. One day, Ruth announced that she was going to make her own rum from a giant marrow. To do this, you cut the top off, dig out all the marrow stuff inside, get brown demerara sugar, ram it in, and put the top back on – that's all! Then you make a hole in the bottom and hang a cup underneath to catch what comes out. As it starts to work the marrow gets sucked in. It's like it's being strangled. The liquid looked a bit like Guinness. You don't get much, but we tried it out in the shed. It took your head off.

'Christ, you can't drink that,' I said. 'You need to mix it with some water, to bring it down a bit.'

Ruth ended up with a whole load of demi-johns in there, all bubbling away.

Eventually, I got going with the house. Unfortunately, I had to put the roof on in the rain, but eventually, I turned a derelict building into a £100,000 property. I did everything, except the electrics, plumbing, and, of course, the plastering.

We lived there for quite a long time, about seven to eight years (from '79 to '87). We moved into the main house during the third year. It took a while because I had to make it habitable first. And there were still lots of things to do after that. It took most of the seven years to do it.

What was I living on, you may ask? Well, just odd jobs. We had some money coming in from the land we rented out for our neighbour's sheep to graze on, and we sold logs from the wood. I used to go down in the woods with the chainsaw. Almost eleven acres of woodland had become overgrown. I guess it hadn't been managed since the 1940s.

The trees were like telegraph poles. So I cut them down in six-foot lengths and sold them for fencing. I couldn't sell them fast enough. I'd typically get four stakes out of a six-foot length of trunk. It was hard work, but it made money. At least I was earning something. I didn't have a profession during this time. I did odd jobs labouring, but I spent most of the time working on the house. I used to buy up old antiques from auctions and restore them at the house. I could make a profit from that too.

Most days, I would take the children to school in the morning and then pick them up in the afternoon. It was a regular routine. Julian went to Llandysul Grammar School. He did very well there. He was a clever boy and won awards. When he was fourteen or fifteen, his teacher asked him to go into a competition; something to do with electronics, maybe called Young Engineer of the Year, that sounds right. The competition was in London, so we booked into a hotel. He submitted a harp with invisible strings. Can you imagine it? He had this thing playing. It was odd, but he'd made it from scratch, all the metal and the batteries. We've still got the remains of it somewhere in the garage. Anyway, he won the competition outright and got a prize. It was money and an offer to go to the university, but he ignored that bit.

The next year, he won it again. He built something else with a computer. It baffled me. Lights were flashing, but apparently, it was quite well-advanced for his age. It just shows how his brain works. Later, he could take a car apart and put it back together. He also speaks fluent Welsh and French. He's an academic and gets that from Ruth. I'm just handy with the practical stuff. I remember a chap at his school telling me that Julian was very clever. I replied that he wasn't so clever, just very annoying, but he did understand electronics. He went to university and did well. We didn't have to pay for that, because in those days the young 'uns got grants.

I used to take Rachel to St Elizabeth's High, or was

Secondary Modern? I can't remember. She was very academic, but just did the job and came home. I used to take her out to discos and this could be quite chaotic. I would drive in the dark around various towns near Carmarthen and I'd get lost. With so many farms and outbuildings there, it was hardly surprising.

Ruth wasn't teaching while we were at College Farm. She was a housewife. I remember that once she wanted a fireplace. So I built a stone one around the pre-existing chimney. When I'd finished it she came in and said, 'Do you mind if I say something? It would look better over there.'

I replied that I was going to kill her and I resisted making any changes for a month. Of course, I gave in. I knew she was right, but why hadn't she said in the beginning? I eventually built a new chimney against an external wall.

She always used to say, 'Can I say something?'

'Well, yes you can, Ruth,' I'd reply.

It took years, but there were nice people around me there. Except for the one farmer, who didn't like me. But, in general, they were okay. Our farm was huge. It ran down from Tanglwst. The farmer had three bungalows built on his land next to the main road. The village itself was called Cwm Morgan. Newcastle Emlyn was quite a nice place and we used to go into Carmarthen to socialise. We made friends anyway and had good contacts there.

I was very friendly with Glyn Davies, who had the fifty acres for his cattle. I used to feed them for him sometimes in the winter. He lived two miles away and couldn't always get across. The cattle would come galloping down in the morning. It was bloody terrifying. I used to stop and just chuck the hay into the field. He had sheep as well. When a sheep goes over on its side, it's sort of flat, and you can't roll it. You try and lift it, and it's like a dead weight. I told him his sheep were bloody-minded and he agreed. He also had a sheepdog. It was English and couldn't understand his Welsh. I asked him why he didn't check this out before he bought it.

We were snowed in once. The wind blew all the snow onto the roads and created a twelve-foot drift. So Glyn lent me his digger and I got most of it out. And then he permitted me to go across his field to get to the main road with my Land Rover. Glyn's neighbour, Mr Butts, I think his name was, got all cross about this, but Glyn put him right. They were arguing like that. Mr Butts was a horrible man and he had three strange sons. It reminded me of the movie *Deliverance*: Three terrible people!

That same winter, A Mr Wylle died. He ran a store in Tanglwst. He had a daughter and she could lift concrete blocks. She was a massive girl. They couldn't get Mr Wylle's body out. So they sent this machine from Carmarthen to dig out the snow. We all followed it down to the cemetery in Carmarthen. We went there in the Land Rover. By the time we came back in the afternoon, the snow was melting. But My Wylle had done us all a favour, enabling us to get out.

Another time, we hosted an exhibition in our house. A guy was selling carpets and we put them out for him and people came from the village. Well, the women went home and told their husbands off after they saw all the work I'd done. Ruth said to one of our neighbours, Mrs Jones, 'You haven't seen the secret door, have you?'

It was a bookcase and it had a hydraulic thing in the back. You pressed it and it opened up and inside was a small anteroom, leading through to another toilet, which you couldn't get to straight from any other main room. Well, Mrs Jones went in there and when she came out, she was green with envy. She said to her husband, 'I want one of those.' He said I was annoying him, but I suggested, even though I'd done ours myself, copied it from a historic building – Pembroke Castle I think – that he had enough money and could pay someone to build him one. It's still there, that secret door.

Lots of people came to the house. We used to take it in turns, driving the kids back and forth from school discos and stuff. That's probably really why I stayed there so long. We truly felt part of the community.

Chapter Seventeen
Holly

There was some bad news. My daughter Rachel abandoned her child Holly and left her with us. She was in university in London at the time and she came home one night and said she was pregnant and that she wanted to give the baby away. Rachel was nineteen and this boy turned up, John James. We all make mistakes, but I told them to sort themselves out, and that I would support them. He told me he'd come back the next day, but he never did.

It was a very traumatic time for us. I had to go up to London to talk to Rachel's professors, because she hadn't been attending her lessons, or studying. She was academic and quite artistic too, but she had no regard for us as her parents. Unbeknown to me, she'd left her university accommodation and moved into a hotel, so I had to go up and speak to the college and they were pretty angry.

We both found it very stressful dealing with Rachel, who came back to live with us leading up to the birth, but Ruth told me that we were taking on the baby. I was happy to do as I was told. Ruth was running the house and doing all the cooking. So we did.

Holly was born in 1985. After this, Rachel did breastfeed and initially nursed her, but she clearly considered the baby a burden. We'd had lots of discussions about giving the baby up for adoption, but Ruth was adamant that we weren't going to do that and, as time went on, we took over completely. We tried getting some assistance from John James and we were offered £1 a week. Ruth remembers that. It was disgusting. How could anyone think you could bring up a child for that? He was working and I found it quite deceitful. But we got over that and we got quite settled in at College Farm and Holly was, of course, growing up. Ruth was quite happy there too. Rachel left and got her own place, but we remained in contact and we would meet up with her.

During this time, I was still working on the house. I would sometimes put Holly to bed, around half past six or seven, whilst Ruth was cooking the evening meal for us. She had a sparkly lamp by her bed that shone stars on the ceiling. I'd sing her a song, and in ten seconds she'd be gone. So I'd close the door quietly then go downstairs and set the cement mixer going, or be working with drills and hammers. I kept checking on her, but she slept all through that.

She was very interested when I was working on the house. She was always behind me. At one point, I was looking for my tape measure, which Holly had posted through a hole in the floorboards. It had dropped down into the cellar underneath. She'd do the same with pencils and hammers. Of course, she was everywhere. Julian had a girlfriend at the time called Karen, or an ex-girlfriend and I remember her once coming into the house and sweeping Holly up in her arms. I thought she'd be nice to have around, but Julian was always moving on. Her surname was Cole, the same as my mother's maiden name. Small world, isn't it?

Chapter Eighteen
Penc Nwc

It was always money with us and wasn't long before we ran out of money again. So we had to sell College Farm in 1987. If I'd had more money I might have been able to hold out and perhaps sell off bits of the land, instead of the entire property, but things had got to a point where I'd started selling our own furniture to make ends meet. It wasn't one particular event, it was just a situation that built up and got worse over time. We were living on next to nothing. So I let it all go in one hit.

I sold it to an American chap from Silicon Valley. He came to the house in a helicopter, landed it on Glyn Davies' land. Mr Davies wasn't too pleased with that, as he hadn't asked permission. This guy tried to say he was on my land and I had to explain to him where the fence line was and that Glyn had cattle on the land he'd put his helicopter down on!

Anyway, as it turned out, he or his son was associated with one of the big antiques auction houses: Bonhams I think, or Sotheby's. Well, they saw all my stuff there and they were eyeing that up. He wanted to look all over the property and was very pushy. I explained where the land extended to and the river and he went off to have a look. I gave him a map. Well, it was hours before he came back, at which point he simply agreed to buy the property. Well, that offended me terribly. He didn't even have a cup of tea. I replied that I'd consider selling it to him, which quite surprised him. So, he asked me how much I wanted for it. I told him. He accepted it, and he did buy the property.

It was a lot of money at the time, £110,000. We made about an £80,000 profit on it.

He gave us very little time to pack up and move out, even though he didn't actually move in to my house for another year. He was very brusque. He upset the neighbours, who were asking me why I'd let him buy the house and saying he wouldn't last long. And, he didn't. Square peg in a round hole there. He was far too abrasive and Glyn didn't like him. He wouldn't help him at all.

We moved to a place called The Limes, a Victorian place in Carmarthen. We went in there in 1987. The Limes was a terraced house on the Esplanade – a posh area, overlooking the river. I thought that being in town would be good for Holly, going to school, at Queen Elizabeth's. It was another derelict place, but I did that up. We bought it from an estate agent called Gareth Schourfield. Another character he was. He turned up and told me if I offered £35,000, which was quite cheap, I would get it. Others were offering more, but he'd told the owner that I wouldn't mess him about.

So I bought it. We took the entire downstairs front rooms out, put in steel girders and made it open plan. Another fireplace went in. It had cellars going down and a kitchen: we did all that. Someone else did the roof for me that time.

Time just started moving on, ticking over. We were there for two years and they were happy times. Holly was a small child then. I thought that living in town would be handy for me and I was trying to think what to do next. Living in town was okay. It was comfortable, but it was boring, so we sold The Limes.

Now, there's a bit of a blank here, which I can't work out. I saw another place, called Garden Cottage in Llandeilo.

It was a nine acre spread, which I liked, and I went down on an open day. There were about twelve people wandering round. Cooke and Arkwright were the agents. They wanted offers in sealed envelopes. I got it, but even though they had agreed to it, when I sold The Limes to move there, I suddenly found that they wanted more money. They weren't accepting my sealed bid, so I had nowhere to go. Gwillym said the sealed bid had no legal standing. I decided not to stop the sale on The Limes. I just said, 'I'll find another place.'

It turned out that a chap there called Thomas Crimble was the one who had bought this Garden Cottage over me. I'd offered about £87,000, but he had offered a hundred and something. I remember a guy I knew, a driver, working for Jewsons. Apparently, Crimble paid cash from a suitcase under the table. You know the type. He drove a white BMW. At the time I had a similar car, with a similar number plate. All of a sudden I've got the police asking me if I'm running drugs up to London. I was an ex-cop. I suggested they find out where the drug money was, seize the property at Garden Cottage and then sell it back to me. They didn't.

Anyway, once again, I had nowhere to live. So I said to Ruth, 'I'll charge around the area.'

I knew all the farmers and they all knew me from the pubs. I spoke to a farmer who had a place called Drwyslewyn, a peculiar name. It was owned by his brother, a veterinary surgeon. He was working in the Midlands and the house was empty. I told the farmer I was desperate and he told me not to worry and that I could have it. I asked for how much? He suggested I rent it from him for £30 a week. It was a three-bedroomed, detached house, with a garage and gardens. I asked if he was sure and he was. He knew his brother would be happy to rent the house out, because he didn't want it left empty. I don't know how long I was there, but Holly went from there to the local school in Llandeilo. I had to rent somewhere to give me some time to breathe. I rented there for a while. But, I started looking again and saw this place called Penc Nwc in White Mill, outside Carmarthen. That was where the pub was that I used to go to called the White Mill Inn.

It was a seven-bedroom house, Victorian, with one and half acres around it. It was on the market for £70,000. I don't really know why we kept moving, but I've always felt a need to move on. I was definitely a restless soul. I think if I'd stayed single I'd be dead by now. But when you have a wife and a family pushing you on you have to find a home for them. It needed doing up, which was ridiculous, but that was okay and things were ticking over nicely.

It was sold to me by Mr Gant, who didn't realise when he sold it to me that the electricity supply was coming to Penc Nwc through his farm and on his meter. He lived up the road in a bungalow. I asked why he'd still got power coming to the house and he said he'd always had it. I stressed that he didn't own the house anymore. It was a bit of a cock-up, but we got over that when he agreed to install a new line, direct to my house, after which we cut off the old one. Nobody liked him. He was a Londoner who'd come down, full of ideas. He wanted to build a bungalow on my boundary. That didn't get off the ground because we objected and he lost out on that. We went to court and they refused. Another time, they were trying to pull a barn down and the whole thing collapsed while they were in it. I thought they were dead. His son ran out, covered in dust and debris.

Next thing, he started cutting down my trees (again on the boundary). They grew very fast, but as they grew he was cutting them down. They were on my land. He then tried to deny the right of way across to my place. The local Scout troupe used to go up there with their flags, and he used to stop them. He had a horse called Red and he'd let it go wild. That would put anyone off going up there. We eventually ended up in court over the trees. He then put a gate up. I picked it up one day and threw it. It was a five bar steel gate.

Admittedly, when he saw me do that and backed off a bit. Anyway, in court the judge said he no longer owned the trees, because he'd sold the property off, and they were now on my boundary. He protested that he'd always cut the trees, but the judge told him off and told him to stop. The next month, he did it again. I couldn't believe it. I spoke to the contractor who was doing the work and he said he was just doing what he was told. But he knew we'd been to court and I said I'd sue him as well, if he carried on. So he didn't do any more. It did happen again though. Back in court, the judge told Mr Gant he'd go to prison if he wasn't careful. But he still did it again. The judge wanted to put him in prison, but I objected. I didn't want the man to go into prison, but what a horrendous attitude.

He used to come into the property too, whilst I was working on it. I couldn't believe it. He would say he was just looking.

'What do you mean. It's my house,' I would say.

Ruth said he had a screw loose and I think she was right. He had a lovely ocean going boat moored in Falmouth. I was interested and I went down one day and saw it. 'Zulu', it was called. It was a beautiful thing, with a black hull, three-masted. It was riding at anchor in the water and corrosion had started round the edges. He didn't ever take it ashore. He just used to row out to it. Someone asked me if I knew the owner and I said I did. They said he was a madman, who bought iron for the rigging instead of brass. Apparently, he walked into the sailing club one day, announced himself as the owner of Zulu and wanted a crew to sail with him to South Africa. He was told to get out.

Anyway, at Penc Nwc I just had to renovate inside, make it all tidy. Initially, I was just buying and selling stuff and we were surviving. Holly was happy there growing up, but still a child of course. She used to bring her friends round. She was like Julian: bright as a spark, mischievous, playful. At first I thought, *My God, I've got another girl now*, but she was the complete opposite to my daughter. She was very loving, even from a very young age and she and I definitely forged a strong bond. I guess I was a bit more experienced, having had two children before, but I was always quite careful with Holly. I did not want her to go the same way as my daughter. That thought terrified me. But, of course, this was before Ruth had her stroke, so we both just got on with it and Holly became more and more attached to us. People do ask how we managed. One of my friends said they would have walked away from it, but you can't. The fact is: we just got on with it.

I remember a play pen I made for Holly, but she never stayed long in it. She was always getting out and running around the sofas in the front room. I'd built an extension where the cows had originally been kept and it had a log fire. I used to spend the evening in there quite happily. Holly enjoyed life and she was very popular at school. She was always reading and she could play the piano as well. So I rented one for her to learn. Her teacher used to come to the house to give her lessons and she got through that in no time. She was so good. Her teacher said we should buy her a piano and a good one. He suggested a Steinway! He was a nice chap, but I think there was an academic way to learning the piano and Holly was just going too fast. She passed all the levels so quickly. In the end we got her another tutor, a young lady, but I forget her name. She took Holly on and brought her right up to the top. She got a Grade A with distinction at the end. She's gone off it a bit now, but the talent was there when she was younger.

I bought her a Bluthner Grand. It cost me about £3,000. Steinway is the best. Bluthner is more a softer thing. We had the room for it – it was massive. We sold it long ago, when there wasn't any room for a grand piano any more. But Holly would get in there and be playing and she tried to teach me, but I was disastrous. I had a go at it. I only knew one song, Ode to Joy. I killed that… der- der- der-der-der. She told me to stop:

‘Grandad,’ she said, ‘just leave that.’

It was like watching a person who can drive and comparing that with a stupid driver. She did teach me a lot about music though. My mother loved music too and it’s in my head today. I’m good at singing, but no good with an instrument. I didn’t sing with Holly when she was young, but we do now. At Christmas, if we go up to York to see her. When she was little, Holly always wanted a tree at Christmas. It didn’t matter whether it was real or plastic. She had one particular thing, a fairy or a robin, that she used to put on the top. We lost that for many years and then suddenly found it again. She’s still got it.

Back then though, when Holly was a child, she joined a choir at school. She had a beautiful voice. And was in the Girl Guides. I went to all the school sports days at Nantgerig School. When she went there she didn’t speak Welsh, but by the time she finished she was top of the class. She used to organise school carnivals too. She was pretty confident, but she could sometimes get worked up and there were a few tantrums too. But, raising Holly and being back in the school environment and so forth, also helped me to come out of my shell more and ultimately feel happier with myself, as I do today. That said, when we were living at Penc Nwc, Ruth and I used to go down to The White Mill Inn and do karaoke and singing – all that nonsense! It was quite a happy time.

However, I decided to get a more substantial income. We were still on speaking terms with Rachel. She said she wanted to do something with her life. I suggested that I could get her set up if she wanted, and she said she was interested in running a restaurant. I thought aye, aye and looking back I probably shouldn’t have done anything. But, she wanted something, so I went to Lloyds Bank and they lent me £80,000 to buy this shop in Carmarthen, which we later called The Cave Coffee Shop. It was actually a hair salon before we bought it, but I’d thought that if Rachel ran a restaurant in part of it. I could set up an antiques business there too.

Those plans all fell through, because she decided she didn't want to do it. Pretty much, as soon as she got the place, she pulled out. I was stuck with a restaurant and an £80,000 loan and I didn't have a bloody clue what to do with that.

I had a woman working there called Sandra. She was the cook and she said she could run the café for me. I agreed. She seemed to know what she was doing and she set up the menus and so forth. Later on, I had had the builders in and converted two floors for an antiques centre, which I used as a space to rent out to other people. I wasn't doing anything and they were paying me rent.

We opened the business as The Cave Coffee Shop in 1993 and, after the conversion, the Antiques Centre opened in 1994. At the time, I was the first in Carmarthen to have an Antiques Centre. It ticked over for a while, but we weren't making any money, just standing still, but more was coming from the antiques side than the shop. We were doing all right. We were ticking over. Then Ruth didn't appear one day. She'd had a stroke...

Chapter Nineteen
Ruth's Stroke

1994 – 2024
"You never knew what was going to happen next…"

On the day of Ruth's stroke in 1994, I was in the Cave Coffee shop, waiting for Ruth to come in, but she didn't turn up. She ran the place and dealt with the money and she was driving then. I asked the staff if they knew where she was, but no one did. I went into town and found the minivan parked up, but no sign of her. I got a phone call from someone, asking if I was Mr Robert Maddocks. They said they were from the Glangwili Hospital and had a lady there who they thought was my wife. They immediately told me she had a stroke. I told the staff in the shop I had to go to the hospital.

I found out that Ruth had been on her way to the shop to see me. Apparently, she'd been to the bank first. Upon leaving she was having her stroke, so she went down to the surgery on the corner. I thought they knew her there, but they didn't. I met one of the doctors later, a Dr Jones, who told me she'd found herself confronted by an unknown lady, who seemed to be suffering some sort of mental condition. So they sent her down to the Mental Care part of the hospital. That was wrong. The diagnosis was wrong.

When I got down there, I found she was in this separate

part of the hospital, away from the main part. All the doors were locked and I had to explain who I was. I went down a corridor and Ruth was all by herself, lying there… and it wasn't my wife I was looking at any more.

I took hold of her, but she'd suffered a Grand Mal seizure. She couldn't speak. I called somebody and told them Ruth shouldn't be there. They replied that I couldn't take her out, as I had to get permission for that. But I had some knowledge of what had happened.

'Fuck that,' I said. 'She's had a stroke! She's not mental!'

I grabbed the trolley, but the doors wouldn't open. They only opened one way. I was banging on the door. I got to a point where I lost it. I opened one door and threatened to take the place apart. I got her out, pushing past these people, across the courtyard and into the main hospital. They knew me and in she went. But, it was too late. If she'd had the right attention in the first half an hour she could have regained a lot. I didn't know what was happening, but she lost her entire face, a leg and her speech. It was terrible.

My wife was in the hospital, but I still had a shop to run and a granddaughter. Despite this, I didn't panic. I thought, *Calm down.* I was talking to myself like an idiot, thinking that I couldn't cope. I do feel it was so wrong what had happened. People said I could sue the pants off them, but I just wanted to get Ruth back.

She eventually came out of it, but we had to go to the hospital many times after. She'd come home some days and I felt like I was walking on egg-shells, because I just didn't know what to do. One day, I arrived back and she'd disappeared! It was a big house, with seven bedrooms and extensive grounds. She was found by a police dog in the garden, lying among some trees.

The police came in and were chatting to me. I explained that I'd always coped as a police officer, but the boot was on the other foot now. They were very helpful.

Another day, I came down and she'd smashed all the

lights on my car. And the washing machine. Oh, what a state. We had a washing machine in the downstairs utility room. She'd gone in there and put an entire packet of soap powder in the machine. The room filled up with bubbles and you couldn't actually find her in there. It's funny now, but it wasn't funny then.

I said to her, 'I think you've got too much soap in there, Ruth.'

Those memories are all a bit of a blur, but I felt that I couldn't trust her with anything. Even now she leaves lights and taps on. She made a cup of tea yesterday and she had cornflakes. She took the teapot and poured the tea over the cornflakes. I couldn't stop her in time. She talks to me, but it's like the normal processes have got jammed.

Going back, when it first happened, she had a very unusual injury. The medics made a decision to send her to a place called Rivermead in Oxford. It's place where they take on unusual cases; people who had been injured, or had a stroke. At the time, Ruth was a bit of a guinea pig. There was a guy there who, as a pilot in the war, had been shot in the head. His injuries were just like an image of my wife's, an almost carbon copy. So they sent her up there to Rivermead and I went up to stay there. I was given a flat to stay overnight in. It was a lovely place and all free of course, but only because they wanted to use her as a guinea pig. She had been a very academic lady and now she was stuck in her own head.

I would stay up there Saturdays and Sundays and come back Monday, back to the house and then scurry to open the shop. As you can imagine, I was very stressed. I came home late one night to the pub in White Mill. My friends, Andrea and Mal, ran it. They were Welsh Valley's people. Andrea was a lovely lady and she prepared a meal for me at half past eleven at night. Andrea and Mal also took Holly off my hands occasionally to help out. Other times she stayed with good friends who had children her own age.

That was okay for a while, but I was then returning late to an empty, seven-bedroom house. I can't really explain how that felt, but I thought it was crazy. Eventually Holly decided she wanted to come back and be with me, and that was marvellous. It supported me to have a ten-year-old there.

My cooking was terrible of course – unbelievable! Holly told me that quite often. I had five main meals for the week, but they weren't very good. There was a lot of chicken involved. She complained a lot about it, but she survived. I look back now and laugh, but it wasn't a wonderful time.

Around ten or eleven years old, Holly asked me if she could go and live with her mother in London. What she meant was that she wanted to visit her and stay with her for a bit. Well, she did do that, but it was chaotic because my daughter had absolutely no idea how to look after a young child. Holly got into her make-up and destroyed all that within minutes. My daughter went berserk. Well, that passed, but Holly did ask again if she could go and live with her. I had to think how to answer that, eventually saying yes, if your mum wants you. Then Holly asked if I would be coming with her. I explained I couldn't because I had to look after Ruth. When I'd explained that I couldn't go with her, she decided she didn't want to go after all. She'd worked out that she was probably better off at our house and that was the end of that. I felt guilty that perhaps I'd stopped her from going to her mother, but she told me quite bluntly, as she got older, 'No, Bobby, you're my dad. It's got nothing to do with her. She abandoned me.'

Ruth was at Rivermead for six weeks and we began to see improvements. They thought it was because she had such an academic brain. One day I was there, she was sitting in this room and she was lecturing. I mean, she had a captive audience. It wasn't as if they could be anywhere else, but still. They said, she'd properly forget that by the next day and was most likely speaking just from memory, but that it also showed she'd still got some control. That said, she didn't really speak again for five years.

I saw lots of people there. Some had had operations that had gone wrong. I was talking to one guy. He was saying that I knew Shirley Bassey. I couldn't remember whether I'd mentioned it, but I said, yes, she was a lovely girl. I told him Ruth was leaving soon, to which he replied that he was happy for her, but wanted her to stay there. He liked her you see and didn't want her to go. I explained that she was getting better. He said that he was doing well too and we talked more about Shirley Bassey and about Wales. His mother came in then and told him it was time for bed. It took two men to get him out of that restaurant and put him to bed. I watched on, horrified. He went out screaming and shouting. His mother came back in and apologised to me. I asked her what the problems were and she explained that he lived each day with the belief that he was going to go home tomorrow, always saying, 'I'm going home tomorrow.' He's probably still there. His mother was at her wit's end and asked me how I coped with everything. I could only reply that we just did, and that there were always other people worse off.

Holly was ten. She was unbelievable. Like I said, she was supportive – an amazing kid. She kept me going. She was probably more in charge than I was. We would go to the school sports days. She liked it there and was popular. She continued with her music and piano. I used to go to all the school things and it was great.

She came home from school one day and I was looking after Ruth. Holly had done a lovely painting of the house, Penc Nwc, a grand painting, which she showed me. It was lovely, with all the windows, the drive and the trees. At the time, all the girls were into *My Little Pony* – toys and stories. Holly had them all over the place and explained that in the picture a pony was in the kitchen, another one upstairs in the bedroom, and 'Grandad Pony' was in the garage. I replied that although this was all very interesting, I couldn't actually see the ponies in the picture, and I asked her where they were.

'Silly, Grandad,' she said. 'The curtains are drawn.' She looked at me as though I was thick. I'm still not sure if she was joking, but it was the way she trapped me in to it.

She'd done another picture, maybe when she was a bit younger, showing my life through the ages. I've still got it somewhere. There I am, all young and handsome at one point and later on, balding and so forth. It was how she saw it.

My daughter reappeared on the scene, wanting to take Holly back. She'd taken up with a man called Barry Fennell. He wanted an easy life and wanted a child, so that he could get a house. My daughter went along with that, but I said it wasn't going to happen. We ended up in court: Maddocks vs Maddocks.

The judge, Michael Evans, looked at me and asked what was going on, with me caring for a wife who had had a stroke and also raising Holly. My daughter wasn't in court, so he instructed that she was to come to court that day and we then discussed things in chambers. So the wig comes off and we're talking now: grandfather to grandfather. The barristers were told to sit down. I'd realised the judge was on my side. In the end he said, 'Listen carefully. Today I'm granting full control, jurisdiction to Mr Maddocks, to look after his granddaughter, because he is the only person I can see able to bring the child up without further aggravation.'

He gave me full control… custody, that's it. It all took less than a day. I thanked him, but he said, 'No, thank you.' A lovely judge he was.

This bloke, Barry Fennel was hanging about outside the court. He was a nasty piece of work. The judge found out who he was and told him to leave the premises.

I had Holly then and she was a bright child and a real comfort to be in the house with. She used to say, 'Don't worry, Grandad.' She calls me Bob now though. I have tried to talk to her about her mother, but she's said no, she doesn't want any contact. Ruth is the same, says she doesn't want to talk about her, she's got no interest; the love has gone.

Anyway, Ruth came through and when she came home from Rivermead, she was a lot better. But it's like you're thinking for two people all the time, even now. It's all the little things: you've got to watch what she's doing. Crossing the road, it's unbelievable, you know. She just goes! I always try and park the car, so that I can get round quickly to get her out.

Chapter Twenty
Beating the Bank

After Ruth's stroke I didn't think I could manage the shop anymore. I borrowed money to keep it going and this stressed me. The shop was in Ruth's name and technically I was unemployed. When I borrowed the £80,000 originally a chap came to the house from the bank – and when they come to your house they say different things to what they say in the bank – it's very devious. I'd told him I wanted to borrow £80,000 and he said okay. He brought some forms and had me sign them at the bottom, assuring me they'd fill in all the details later. He'd offered me the money that I wanted, so I just signed it. But after Ruth's stroke, the insurance company, Black Horse, said the business was in my name. I said no, it's in Ruth's name… and she's had the stroke, not me. The business insurance was supposed to cover the £80,000, but the insurers refused to pay.

I called my solicitor to help me out. He was called Gwillym Richards and was based in Newcastle Emlyn. He was a lovely guy. He'd helped me buy my houses. He sat down with me. I explained that Ruth should have a claim on the business insurance, to cover the loan on the shop, which clearly she now couldn't run.

He rang the bank and they passed him back and forth, from Mr Smith to Mr Jones to Mr Evans. It went on like that for ages, passing me round and round to try and lose me.

They said my name was on the form as the owner of the business, which was wrong. I replied that I'd never seen the form. Anyway, it went to court, after Gwillym served notice on them. Gwillym thought there was about a sixty per cent chance of winning the case. I was sure it was all wrong, but he said that courts could see things differently. I understood where he was coming from, so we took them on.

In court, it all came to light. The judge showed me the papers and asked if it was my form. I explained that it wasn't my writing, even though it was my signature on it. The bank had filled it in and swapped it all around, so it was in my name, not Ruth's. Ruth should have been down as the buyer of the shop and the business owner, but they'd transferred the ownership into my name. They'd also put on it that I was on a £25,000 a year salary, which was completely wrong. This was all nonsense. Basically, they'd falsified the paperwork.

So it moved to a big court case in London: 'No win, no fee,' Gwillam told me, although I was paying him. I was terrified to be in court. I mean, I'd been pretty scared when I was a police officer. I just bluffed it through. You feel like once you're in there, you're never going to come back out again.

When the judge looked at the case, he said it was all nonsense and we were able to prove that the bank had switched the title around and the documents were wrong. I'd signed a blank form, the one that had been presented to me when the guy from the bank came to the house.

The judge then asked me, 'Why did you sign a blank form?'

Feeling a bit of an idiot, I replied, 'Well, I was borrowing £80,000 from the man. I'm not going to upset him, am I?'

The judge listened to that and asked my solicitor why he was representing me instead of a local representative. So Gwillym told him that he'd known me for almost thirty years and that, though I might be a bit naïve, I was just a normal guy. He reinforced my testimony that I would simply have trusted the bank manager. They adjourned for lunch, came back in and the judge, Mr Moncaster said right away, 'Pay Mr Maddocks. You'll pay Mr Maddocks today!'

He said the bank were "vicariously responsible" – a big word, essentially because they were present in my house when I signed the document. He said I'd signed the documents in good faith. Their barrister jumped up, but the judge told him to sit down. I liked that judge. I felt like I could kiss him. After all, it had cost £13,000 just to get to court.

Coming back on the train from Paddington after we'd won, Gwillym was sitting there with his briefcase open, looking like Alistair Sim. I got the Guinness in and toasted, saying, 'We did it, Gwillym,' but he corrected me and said it was our barrister that had won the day. Gwillym died about ten years ago, on 8th March. He was a brilliant man.

Ruth asked me what had happened. She hadn't been in court herself because our barrister had said she wouldn't be a reliable witness, as she was just as likely to say yes when she meant no, or one after the other. And it would have been embarrassing for her. I told her we'd won the case. Lloyds Bank had to cover the losses, not the insurers. I found out then that Black Horse Insurers and Lloyds Bank were two different companies. I didn't know that then. The insurers were in the basement and the bank in the top of the same building and that's how they organised switching things around. But the judge said Lloyds Bank was nothing to do with Black Horse. I eventually got most of my money back, about £65,000 in the end, after costs, and we moved on again. But, the whole process took seven years, because when you're up against people who have got lots of money; they just keep deflecting you. But we took them on and we beat them. Not me, but my solicitor and my barrister. I've got no regard for Lloyds Bank now or for any bank really.

Chapter Twenty-One
Property Portfolio

In 1995 I sold the Cave Café/antiques business for a small profit. I just couldn't do it anymore and we needed to get some money in. Then in '97, I sold Penc Nwc. There's a gap there, which I can't really explain, but I do know we moved to Elm Lodge, which I definitely bought in 1998. Around the same time, I bought another run-down property, 2 Conduit Lane. It was a horrible little three-bedroom terraced house. We lived there while I was doing up Elm Lodge. I got Conduit Lane for £35,000. I did it up quite quickly and sold it on for £110,000, so it was worth it. At last, I was getting somewhere in life. That money eventually went into the property we have today.

Elm Lodge was a Georgian house on the Parade in Carmarthen. It had seven bedrooms. I remember Holly sometimes had her friends to stay there, and she was in her teens then. I'd get up to go to the bathroom in the morning and there would be six other girls lined up outside, waiting to use it. I didn't know who the hell they were. Fortunately, there was another bathroom on the ground floor!

We were in Elm Lodge for about ten years. It was a nice, big, rambling house. It was very posh, on what they call the Esplanade. It had a big garage at the back and formal gardens, with two bathrooms like I said, and a library and piano room. It was unbelievable. It probably looked like we'd won the pools. It belongs to a Housing Association now. It's been turned into a residential retirement home. They've ripped the heart out of it. The shell is still there, but the inside is all modern.

In 2000, I started with the buy-to-lets: something I understood. Buy it, do it up, rent it out, make a profit. I'd had my fill of trying to make a profit from restaurants and food. I knew the landlords and estate agents in Carmarthen. This was partly because Holly, during the school holidays, used to work for Terry Thomas Estate Agents. She was very valuable to the business because she could speak Welsh fluently. She would sit at the front desk and no one argued with her! I'd also bought The Limes from Terry Thomas a few years before. Anyway, they knew me and recommended a property at 16 Park Terrace in Carmarthen.

I was borrowing money again. I thought it was a good idea at the time. I borrowed about £3,000 for a deposit for that house and took out a Buy-to-Let mortgage, from Bristol & West. It was a big, four-bedroom house, with gas central heating and a cellar. It didn't need a lot of work. It backed onto the park, where families could go and sit in the sun. It was on the market for around £30,000, maybe £32,000 and looked to be a good investment. I got the mortgage, put the tenants in and off I went. It was fantastic: the rent covered the mortgage payments and I had an income coming in.

About a year later, Terry Thomas told me that number 4 on the same street was coming on the market. He asked me if I wanted to buy it. Initially, I said I hadn't got the money, but he worked it out and showed me that I had, moving money between properties to have enough for another deposit. I lost control of what was happening, but he told me I should go ahead and buy it and then I'd have another income coming in. I went to look at it and my offer was accepted. It was cheap, about £20,000. It had a tree growing in the back, which I had to sort out before I could put tenants in. I put gas in too and all that went very well.

So, now I also own 4 Park Terrace.

Then number 5 came up, followed by 6 and 7. Then, around the corner, I bought 2 Picton Court and17 Trevaughn Road. I put my daughter in that one. She went in there and she was paying rent, but at least it was someone I knew. After that, I bought 42 Trevaughn Road. It was just outside Carmarthen. They called me "Mad Maddocks" at the time, but these buy-to-lets were providing my income. Don't forget that it was very little cost for me to do them up, because I could still do most of it myself.

Then I bought 6 Old Priory Road in Carmarthen. Attached to this house was a large garage, which at the time was owned by an electrical firm. I'd been there one day when they were changing the old wooden doors, which were rotten, for a steel roller door. I'd had a look inside then. I rang them up and they knew me. They said they'd sell it for £20,000 and I thought that was okay. I paid cash. I don't know where the cash came from, but the income from all the other properties meant that I was comfortable, for the first time in life. When I had several properties I was making a profit of about £1,000 each month. I felt I was getting on and moving up, and, of course, from age 65 I was also getting an old age pension. We'd maybe also sell a property now and then to get a lump sum in. It all worked out well.

When I was buying the garage, David Owen came on the scene. He had previously bought Penc Nwc from me. He was a big man, with a lot of properties. He came into town and bought another house adjacent to the garage. He went to the electricians and, told them he knew me and that I wouldn't mind. He said he'd offer them more money: £25,000. They rang me up asking about him. I said they could do what they liked. They could take his money, but I wouldn't be speaking to them again. But because we'd already shaken hands on a deal, they confirmed it was mine. David Owen was really upset. He just denied that he'd tried to scupper my deal. Anyway, I bought the property. My son thought this was a good idea and moved in there rapidly with four cars. They're still there: all in a state of disrepair. He's got a BMW 635, with the registration BMW 635. It's amazing. There's no income from it as he doesn't pay rent. He's very good with cars, you see, and he could restore them, but he's got no time. I've told him to sell the cars, so I can sell the garage and have some cash again, but he doesn't seem to think that I really want to get out. He's up in bloody Oxford. He comes down occasionally. It'll be worth about £100,000 after I'm dead!

I bought all those properties in the early 2000s and I've now got two left. I sold the others off. The agents collected the rent and paid it into my bank account. I also had money from the council tenants. I didn't always get the full amount from these people. It was hard for some of them. I've had a lot of characters in those houses over the years: a cannabis grower, who went to prison in the end. The house stank of it and because I'd got numbers 4, 5 and 6, the smell permeates through the lofts you see. It was his neighbours who said there was cannabis next door, and the electricity and water bills were very high.

He was just one of many people. Others kept their motorbikes in the front room, where they would change the oil! Some were aggressive, but I was quite tough in those days and you could get people out quite easily then, but not anymore. You could tell people, 'If you don't get out, I'll throw you out.' If they were druggies, you could work on their Achilles heel.

As my mate Glen said, 'If they threaten to call the police, I tell them to go ahead because the police will find cannabis there.' Sometimes they protested and said that Glen was going to plant the stuff. He'd reply, 'Of course, I'm going to plant it. I suggest you go now." And they would.

Looking back, I should really have bought, done them up, and re-sold all the properties. I'd recommend to anyone: don't get involved with tenants. You can't get people out.

You have to go to court. I wouldn't recommend anyone do it. It's a lot of stress.

In the end, I sold them because there were just too many people to manage. Sometimes of course, they would let their mates stay, on a semi-permanent basis, and you'd find people sleeping on the sofa. They could be rude and arrogant. They were staying in the house for free, or very cheaply. I turned up to one and he asked who I was. I said, 'I'm the landlord. Bloody hell.' I kicked him out.

Another time, in a house with only one tenant, mail was arriving for five names. They were probably using the address to run some sort of scam. To be honest, I probably only had three or four good tenants in all that time. One girl was a vet. She used to have window cleaners to come and clean the windows, and she washed them and she did the guttering. I was amazed. Nobody usually bothers. She had a cat too. I used to see it in the garden. One or two of the others kept the place tidy, never complained and appreciated they had a good landlord. I didn't bother them and if there was something wrong, my mates Glen and Marco would generally sort it for me and send me the bill. They lived nearby and they did general house maintenance. They did look after me. Marco is Italian. They are both craftsmen. Watching them put in windows is unbelievable. They're so quick. You know: measure it, whack it in. That's it!

When we had to tidy a place or clear it out, we would use my van to take everything down the tip. Then we'd go to the pub afterwards, of course.

Marco said, 'Every time we go there we always end up in the pub.'

Glen said, 'Yes, it's getting that I can't afford it.'

They did fight. Glen was a hard man, very temperamental. You didn't mess with him! Marco is great. It's a business though and it's a lot of worry, with people misbehaving and sometimes damaging the property. One tenant had a rabbit in the house and the rabbit ate the carpet.

They'll eat anything, rabbits. I saw it through the window. It was like a railway track. At first, I thought it was something on the floor, but he'd just nibbled all through it.

It was difficult to manage it all. Saying that, I've made a profit selling them off. Not a lot, by the time you've paid capital gains, but yes, some. I've got two left now. One I can hopefully sell next year. The other one is occupied by my mate Simon and he wants to buy the house off me. He's a bit eccentric and he's fearful of Ruth. He's a great guitar player, but he can't sing and Ruth told him in front of everyone, 'Don't sing, Simon.' His father is ninety-eight and Simon's hoping he might leave him some money. I said he shouldn't be waiting for his dad to die, but he said, 'Come on, Bob, he's ninety-eight!' That's not nice, is it? It's the way he says it. But then my buy-to-let days will be over. In another year or two, they'll all be gone.

Chapter Twenty-Two
A Bit More About Holly

Holly went to Warwick University. She was happy to move away from home, even though I'd suggested maybe Cardiff. She was independent-minded. In the end, she got a doctorate. She speaks languages and she lectures now to hundreds of people.

She doesn't have children. She and her partner are career people. She goes through life so fast. I think someone should slow her down. They live in a big house and built an extension on it. I suggested she buy a cheaper one, but she said she was not doing what I did. Apparently, she might be leaving the house for six months and coming to stay with me.

I've sat in an auditorium in Oxford, with all these people from America. There must have been a hundred and fifty people there. I was there with my son Julian and Ruth. They introduced her, Holly Naomi Jane Maddocks, and went through all her qualifications and I thought, *Is that my granddaughter?* Apparently, she's a highly respected authority on Medieval English. I was looking around and they were all impressed. She starts off with a Welsh lilt, but that disappears and she gets a bit posh.

This lady next to me says that she's from Houston and had come over specifically "to listen to this young lady."

'Oh,' I said, 'That's interesting. She's my granddaughter.'

Well, I was suddenly important then and I said, 'I've taught her all I know.'

Anyway, she's a bit like me in one way: she's got the brains. She held those people in the palm of her hand. Pictures were rolling up on the screen. I was baffled by what she was talking about: beautiful, coloured manuscripts, she knows all about them and the scribes and their little techniques. She found an unknown one and she's writing a book on it now. It's not a novel. It's an academic book. But it'll be the go-to book, like the police manual: *Moriarty's Police Law* – you've got to buy it.

It's a different world she inhabits, but she's the apple of my eye, you know that.

Chapter Twenty-Three
The Final Move… Probably

Although we lived for a long time in West Wales, we were from Penarth and we used to see old friends in Dinys Powys. One day, as we went through Cowbridge, Ruth asked if I fancied coming back to my home town. Well, most of the people I knew there were dead, but as we came through, Ruth saw this advert in Herbert R Thomas, Estate Agents. The notice was peeling off their wall and it looked like nobody wanted the place.

It was a derelict sixteenth of seventeenth century gatehouse to a castle. It was stone built and freezing cold. You can't make it up, can you? I mean, who wants that? But Ruth liked it. We went in to the agents and had a chat about it.

I didn't mind the idea of coming back to Penarth and I'd go anywhere Ruth wanted to go. I'd go back to Australia. Well, maybe we're a bit too old for that. But, I didn't feel too old to be doing up a property again. I was still quite fit. Ruth wanted it badly and nobody else wanted it. When we viewed it, there were maybe seven other people there, wandering around. We came away and Ruth said to leave it because there were too many other people interested. We walked away, but then we got a phone call from Herbert Thomas. They'd had no offers.

I bought the place in 2008, for about £10,000 less than

the asking price, as they couldn't sell it. I said, 'Here we go again, Ruth.'

We took a mortgage out with Northern Rock, quite a big one. I think it was about £320,000 at the start, but we've chipped away at it. It's been going down and down and I've got £49,000 left, I think. Still a lot of money, but its approachable. If I kick my son out of the garage, I can get £70,000 for that! It's all paid for. I've told Julian if he gives me £5,000, I'll sign over the deeds. But he'll get it all when I'm gone.

Northern Rock collapsed, of course, and what a nightmare that was.

We didn't move in for a year or two, maybe longer. We stayed in Elm Lodge while I did it up. The driving down was annoying. It took about an hour each way. I ended up going into the pub a lot of the time. I was so exhausted. But it helped because I met the plumber and the roofer there. I mostly went back every night, but I did sleep at the gatehouse one night. It was horrible: a big empty house and it was freezing cold. In the morning I had breakfast and thought, 'Ha, I'm going home.' I was fit, but I was elderly. We haven't actually lived in there that long. Ruth is trapped in her head – in a world of her own. When we're in the house together and it's just me and her. Well, she's got no one else to talk to. She's got the washing machine about sorted, but I do all the cooking and the running about, and the driving, of course. And I do all the money. I wear glasses to drive. I was an advanced driver in the police force. I never used to get nervous driving, but I'm older and now it's not easy with Ruth alongside me. She'll suddenly shout, 'Go left there!'

Sometimes she will try to get out on the wrong side. I'd tell her, 'Don't open the door the traffic side. Wait until I've turned round, but she does it anyway. No one will stop. They'll take the bloody door off.' By the time we get out the car, we'll be arguing.

I've done it for the last thirty years, but my cooking isn't very good. My granddaughter complains. I started cooking for her when she was young and I had just five main meals. There was a lot of chicken and rice and some fish, and I did blend things a bit. I'd put it all in together. She ate it! My mother was a very good cook. You forget how good they were years ago. They used to buy food every day didn't they, and bring it home; there was no refrigeration. Pasta is easy and I do pies and garlic bread. But it's timing with me. I burn stuff or forget to add the sauce at the right time. But you've got to do it and I've had to learn. Ruth will sit down and say she's not hungry, but then eat the lot! Sometimes she does leave half of it. I don't like chucking stuff away though.

Ruth and I have been married for sixty years. I was twelve when I first went to her house on my paper round and I guess we first began dating when I got back from sea the first time, around seventeen. We didn't have a big do for that sixtieth anniversary. My son came down and we went for a meal out. That's all you want, isn't it? We went down to the jetty in Penarth that I'd worked on, The Custom House. The jetty is still there, but it's pretty level with the water now. There used to be a forty-foot drop when the tide went out. That's the depth of the water there now. It's where the water taxis come in.

We don't visit Penarth so much now. We go to the auction house in Penarth Road and occasionally into town. But Ruth doesn't like Cardiff much anymore now. It's too busy. Too many cars and people shouting and bawling in the street. It's not my scene either, is it? One bloke was shouting at the wall once and I asked him if he was all right. Of course, you shouldn't speak to anyone, should you? He turned around and what he called me I don't know. I just said, '...and good day to you 'n all.'

I was told I shouldn't talk to people. I asked what was wrong with this guy and was told he was likely on drugs. It's crazy. Where are the police? There are no police. Nobody moves them on. I saw an elderly couple sitting there and others were effing and blinding and ranting at them. It's not normal. Penarth is quieter. Penarth's all right, but Cardiff! I'd go and join the police force there, if they'd have me in, but they wouldn't.

In Penarth, all the properties I lived in are still standing. I know them all: I know all the prices: what was a £500 house is now £250,000. All the houses I've ever bought are still there too, although the neighbourhoods have changed. I went to a house in St Augustine's Crescent, after a funeral. There were nine houses there and I didn't know which one it was so I knocked on them all. They were occupied by people of all different nationalities. I didn't have a clue. They were all posh, all educated and, of course, lots of cars parked outside. I got to the end and hadn't found it. It turned out he was number 1. I'd started the wrong way, at number 9.

In Carmarthen, you can go to The Limes today. It's still there. A doctor bought it from me, and then another doctor bought it from him. There are some characters in Carmarthen. I'm losing contact with them all now, but they were all working people and we used to do stuff together. David Owen sold on Penc Nwc. The coffee shop is still there, with a change of name.

Last week I was ill. I woke up early on a Saturday morning. I was looking outside and it was light, but then when I looked again it was getting darker. Ruth had got up too and asked me what was happening and I told her it was getting darker. In truth, it was nine o'clock at night that we'd woken up. We had slept all through the day. I asked Ruth, who wasn't ill, why she had and she said she'd just stayed there with me, to keep me company. Maybe she thought I might have gone. Anyway, it was nine o'clock at night and I wanted to get up. I asked her what we should do. We had some breakfast, or supper, whichever, and just went back to bed.

It was crazy. It was my son's birthday on that Saturday. He was out in Qatar at the time. I did tell him we'd slept for twenty-four hours. He said we needed seeing to!

I've had an interesting life. The best job I ever had was in the police. You never knew what was going to happen next, a bit of a motif for my life really. Okay, in the Prison Service in Australia I carried a Winchester rifle, but the inmates were all pretty happy being in there. It was mainly an open prison, with people who were there for maybe two weeks for non-payment of their rent. There was a farm they worked on that was part of the complex, although it was miles away and I never actually went there. There were about three hundred inmates during my time. There were some serious criminals that were in there for life.

The Merchant Navy gave me lots of experience and helped me grow up quickly and seeing foreign parts, not in a book, but for real, that was quite something. But I was nervous as hell when I joined the police force. I wanted to do it right. I learned the law and came top in the exam. I thought if I got it right then it would help hide my lack of self-confidence. Mind you, after that exam, when it was reviewed, my results got mixed up with 401 and he got all the praise. He didn't say anything.

We were mixed up quite a lot, we were, being 401 and 402. He was a lazy sod though. Some officers just wanted a quiet life. He refused to examine the body the first time we attended a death together. I'd already done a few. I said that he had to do it because the Coroners Court would ask him about it. It was clear the chap had died, but we had to determine there were no visual signs of assault or anything else. I told him that I wasn't going to lie for him in court and say he'd examined the body. He was a nice guy, but he was very lazy. I was working all the time.

Every time I tried to sit down to write a report, the alarm went off again, all the time. The engine in the car I had never stopped, except for that time when the gear stick came off. Shifts were six to two, two to ten, and ten to six. You'd be picking people up all the time. You'd put a "Police-Stop" sign up in the road. A lot of people didn't like to stop because they thought that if you were stopped you'd be in trouble. I didn't want trouble. I just wanted the criminals, you see. But I would chat to people and often you'd discover that they didn't have a licence or insurance, but those things were nothing and I would suggest for them to sort it out the next day, and I'd let them off. But if you stopped them a week later and they still hadn't done it, well then you'd have them. But you give people a chance, especially on Christmas Eve. I didn't book anybody on Christmas Eve.

One Christmas Eve, there was a nurse's home on twelve beat and outside it was a Police Box. They were having a party and they were all shouting and encouraging me to go in and join them. I had the car, but they said I should bring the car in. I took the car into the compound. I told them I couldn't have a drink, but we were all part of the same business, weren't we? So, I had half a shandy with them, but then said I had to go. I was asked where I'd got to, so I said I'd just been checking on something. You had to be able to lie quickly. We had a lot of fun.

Policing isn't the same today. Police officers don't seem to know how to talk to people. Look at all those riots in London. You can't arrest twenty thousand people, can you? Mind you, people today are very rude to the police too. Someone could give an officer the finger and that would constitute an offence now. It's described as an assault: an offer to do injury one to the other. But you can talk to people. I only ever used my truncheon once. I hit a bloke on his arm.

I reckon all the best years are gone, especially with what's happening now in the Middle East. It's terrifying. People are shouting terrible stuff in the streets here. But you can't say too much in the pub. People should get out in the world a bit and see what life's about. Going to sea, you learn fast.

I'm now in a property that I owe only £45,000 on and it's probably worth £500,000. I'm not going to move again, not until I go to the mortuary. It'll go to my son and I guess my granddaughter will have something. We've been collecting antiques for so many years, our house is absolutely stuffed full of them; it's like a museum. On paper I'm maybe worth a lot, but I'm still always short of money. My son always tells me not to worry about money, but I do worry about it. He does look after me now, but I don't want his money. I came from nothing; my father had nothing.

We never know what's around the corner. We're all born with different personalities and different strengths. I keep telling people, 'I was a very quiet and shy person when I was younger,' but even then people seemed to think I was mature for my age. However, you do end up doing exactly what you don't want to do sometimes and still making a success of it. For me, that was on the ships and in the police force. Maybe it was all my jobs. But I had responsibility and those jobs helped me to get over my shyness. Okay, I did it my way, but I tried to do the jobs the way they were expected to be done. In the end, people tended to leave me alone to just get on with the job.

We've become a bit soft today. People are forever going on the sick. I had to work, even when I was ill. I had to, to provide for my family.

Funny thing is, if the police had accepted me in Cardiff, I might have stayed there my whole working life. Some people are very happy being at home their whole lives. You can visit anywhere now, of course, on a plane. But when you do that it's a holiday and when you're on holiday you're not really seeing the place and the people as it should be. I liked getting out and seeing the real people. In the ships, I saw people carrying iron ore on their backs, like ants, and you realise how lucky you are. In Australia I saw the aborigines and how they lived.

We're still waiting on the pensions from our time in Australia. My accountant has sent letter after letter. To begin with, they denied knowing me, or that I was there.

We're established here now in Cowbridge. I do see my son and granddaughter in York and Oxford. For the last twelve years or so, I've mostly spent my time in the local pubs, chatting to people. I suppose I could go to church every day, like some people do. Or, I could join the local gym, but I can't do that, with my back: I'd kill myself. Time was, I couldn't go out and didn't drink because I didn't have any money. It was work, work, and work.

I think, truthfully, the work that's given me the most satisfaction was doing up the houses. I was in a world of my own, talking to myself, knowing that I was making money and keeping my Mrs happy! And getting knowledge about those seventeenth century houses – how they built them. It was clever, especially the fireplaces. They were well thought out and, of course, built of stone.

I don't have to work for a living anymore; but I do go to the antiques sales at the auction houses. I have an eye for what's valuable and I can restore seventeenth century furniture. I did that in Australia too. I was a registered restorer and valuer. I prefer wood, not metal. It's more forgiving, and you can have a rest in between. God knows where that came from, my father probably.

I look after Ruth every day, which is more than I could ever have realised. Ruth gets in a very strange mood some days. She doesn't realise she's doing it, and she often has no regard for other people's feelings. I have to bring her back. Look at today. We went out to buy bird food: £15 on bird food, every week. I said, 'Ruth, that's £60 a month.' How did they manage, when I wasn't around? They survived didn't they? But now: we're paying to feed the birds, the bloody crows come down and take most of it. They fly off into the woods and our neighbour shoots them. We had a row about that today. Though she's gone all quiet again now. That £60 could be spent on Guinness – its £5 a pint now!

We don't have a proper conversation, because Ruth can't get all the words out. It's not her fault.

Ruth and I go to karaoke. I sing all the songs, do Elvis and Tom Jones so on, and Roger Whitaker;

There's a ship lies rigged and ready in the harbour tomorrow, for old England she sails…

And I shall be aboard that ship tomorrow…

And it goes on:

For you are beautiful and I have loved you dearly more dearly than the spoken word can tell.

That goes down well because they all join in with: *For you are beautiful.* They're all going then and I can relax and not sing.

The joke when we get up on the stage is, we say, 'We're not getting paid for this, you know.'

And they reply, 'Thank God!'

I've told Ruth we might have to move again, because of the stairs, into a bungalow. She says she's not moving again, but what I meant was a longhouse. In the old days, in a Welsh longhouse the animals would be in one end. Thing is, I think those stairs, where we are now, will be the end of both of us. But I guess it's a problem I'll deal with in due course.

Of course, my relationship, or lack of one with my father, is something I regret. Ruth still remembers what she said to him. She cannot forget that my father was the rudest and most ignorant man she'd ever met and she couldn't believe he had a son like me. She wasn't a shrinking violet, was she? That's why I married her, I think. Some girls were silly or only interested in make-up and stuff and I remember one asked me about The Beatles. I didn't know who they were. I wasn't really interested. I knew of Tom Jones. I think he's the same age as me and he's been pretty successful in his life.

I don't have any other regrets. I mean, I wish I'd been born into a multi-million-pound family. No, not really. That wouldn't allow you to make yourself what you are: you have to do it yourself.

I proved to myself that I could be successful, and against all the odds, I think. My son says I don't look my age, but I reply that I do bloody feel it.

But, I've always tackled things with enthusiasm and it's what you make it.

That's just life.